LOW FAT
Sauces

LOW FAT
Sauces

Consultant Editor
LINDA FRASER

southwater

This edition is published by Southwater

Distributed in the UK by
The Manning Partnership
251–253 London Road East
Batheaston
Bath BA1 7RL
UK
tel. (0044) 01225 852 727
fax. (0044) 01225 852 852

Distributed in the USA by
Ottenheimer Publishing
5 Park Center Court
Suite 300
Owing Mills MD 2117-5001
USA
tel. (001) 410 902 9100
fax. (001) 410 902 7210

Distributed in Australia by
Sandstone Publishing
Unit 1, 360 Norton Street
Leichhardt
New South Wales 2040
Australia
tel. (0061) 2 9560 7888
fax. (0061) 2 9560 7488

Distributed in New Zealand by
Five Mile Press NZ
PO Box 33-1071
Takapuna
Auckland 9
New Zealand
tel. (0064) 9 4444 144
fax. (0064) 9 4444 518

Southwater is an imprint of
Anness Publishing Limited
© 1997, 2000 Anness Publishing Limited

1 3 5 7 9 10 8 6 4 2

Publisher: Joanna Lorenz
Consultant Editor: Linda Fraser
Assistant Editor: Margaret Malone
Recipes: Catherine Atkinson, Nicola Diggins, Christine France, Sue Maggs,
Annie Nichols, Liz Trigg and Steven Wheeler
Designers: Kim Bale, Visual Image, Peter Butler, Bob Gordon,
Peter Laws, Alan Marshall and Keith Brambury
Photographers: William Adams-Lingwood, Edward Allwright,
James Duncan, Michelle Garrett, Don Last and Peter Reilly

Previously published as *Step-by-step Low Fat Sauces*

Printed and bound in China

For all recipes, quantities are given in both metric and imperial
measures, and, where appropriate, measures are also given in standard
cups and spoons. Follow one set, but not a mixture, because they are
not interchangeable.

CONTENTS

INTRODUCTION

A delicious sauce, whether served as an accompaniment or as an integral part of a dish, can transform the plain and ordinary into something really exciting. Sauces can also, however, introduce an unwelcome amount of fat into a recipe. It is a common question – how do you cut down on fat without sacrificing flavor? *Low Fat Sauces* solves this by providing a wealth of fabulous low fat recipes with tips and techniques on quick and easy low fat cooking methods.

Traditionally, sauces frequently include dairy products, such as butter, cream, milk and cheese, or are made with oil and eggs, as in mayonnaise. Sauces made with such ingredients will be high in fat and calories. However, supermarkets now offer a huge selection of reduced fat products that provide ideal alternatives. Yogurt, skim or semi-skim milk, half fat crème fraîche, reduced-fat spreads and lower-fat soft cheeses like ricotta can all be effortlessly substituted in recipes with delicious, lighter results.

Low fat sauces may also be based on fresh, flavorsome stocks, or fruits and vegetables, cooked if necessary, then puréed or strained for a smooth consistency. Fragrant fresh herbs, tangy citrus juices, exotic spices and a range of pantry ingredients can all be used to create new and imaginative low fat sauces.

Whatever the occasion, from weekday meals to parties and informal entertaining, and whether you need a speedy dip to serve as an easy appetizer or a light snack, a tasty sauce to jazz up fish, meat, poultry, pasta or vegetables, an exciting Mexican-style salsa accompaniment, or a pretty fruit coulis for a tempting dessert, you'll find an enticing and low fat version here.

Do We Need Fat in Our Diet?

We only need 10 g fat in our daily diet for our bodies to function properly. A totally fat-free diet would be almost impossible to achieve, since some fat is present in virtually every food.

A certain amount of essential fatty acids are necessary in our diet to help our bodies absorb vitamins A, D, E and K as they are fat-soluble and cannot be made by the body. Fat is also needed to make hormones. Recent research has proved that we all eat far too much fat. Doctors now recommend that we limit our fat intake to no more than 30% of our total daily calorie intake, even as low as 25% for a really healthy diet. Some fats in the diet are a contributory factor in heart disease and breast, prostate and colon cancers.

Types of fat in foods

Saturated fats are hard fats found in meat, most dairy products, such as butter, cream, margarine, cheeses and animal fats. Palm and coconut oil are also high in saturated fats. Saturated fats can raise the blood cholesterol level and clog up the arteries. The way we prepare and cook foods can limit the amount of saturated fat that we consume.

Polyunsaturated fats are soft fats such as sunflower, safflower, and corn oils, and fish such as mackerel, salmon or herring and nuts, seeds, cereals, lean meats and green vegetables. These fats may help to reduce our cholesterol levels.

Mono-unsaturated fats should make up most of the fat in our diet. They appear to have a protective effect and help lower cholesterol levels. Olive oil, peanut oil and avocados are all rich sources of mono-unsaturated fats.

A selection of foods containing the three main types of fat found in foods.

Eating a Healthy Low Fat Diet

Eat a good variety of different foods every day to make sure you get all the nutrients you need.

1 Skim milk contains the same amount of calcium, protein and B vitamins as whole milk, but a fraction of the fat.
2 Low-fat yogurt, cottage cheese and ricotta cheese are all high in calcium and protein, and are good substitutes for cream.
3 Starchy foods such as rice, bread, potatoes, cereals and pasta should be eaten at every meal. These foods provide energy and some vitamins, minerals and dietary fiber.
4 Vegetables, salads and fruits should form a major part of the diet, and about 1 lb should be eaten each day.
5 Eat meat in moderation but eat plenty of fish, particularly oily fish such as mackerel, salmon, tuna, herring and sardines.

A few simple changes to a normal diet can reduce fat intake considerably. The following tips are designed to make the change to a healthier diet as easy as possible.

Meat and poultry
Red meats such as lamb, pork and beef are high in saturated fats, but chicken and turkey contain far less fat. Remove the skin before cooking and trim off any visible fat. Avoid sausages,

A selection of foods for a healthy low-fat diet.

burgers, pâtés, bacon and minced beef. Buy lean cuts of meat and skim any fat from the surface of stocks and stews.

Dairy products
Replace whole milk with skim or 1% milk and use low-fat yogurt, low-fat sour cream or ricotta cheese instead of cream. Use cream, cream cheese and hard cheeses in moderation. There are reduced-fat cheeses on the market with 14% fat content which is half the fat content of full fat cheese. Use these wherever possible.

Spreads, oils and dressings
Use butter, margarine and low-fat spreads sparingly. Try to avoid using fat and oil for cooking. If you have to use oil, choose olive, corn, sunflower, canola and peanut oils, which are low in saturates. Look out for oil-free dressings and reduced-fat mayonnaise.

Hidden fats
Muffins, cakes, pastries, snacks, chips, and processed meals all contain high proportions of fat. Get into the habit of reading food labels carefully and looking for a low-fat option.

Cooking methods
Grill, poach and steam foods whenever possible. If you do fry foods, use as little fat as possible and pat off the excess after browning, with paper towels. Make sauces and stews by first cooking the onions and garlic in a small quantity of stock, rather than frying in oil.

Flavorings for Low Fat Sauces

Sauces don't have to be rich in fat, like the classic mayonnaise, hollandaise and béchamel, or prepared using generous amounts of oil and butter. Take a closer look at the range of readily available ingredients you can use to produce delicious low fat versions.

To compensate for the lack of fat in the form of butter, oil, cream and full-fat cheeses, the recipes in this book make good use of the rich flavors of concentrated sauces, onions, garlic, fresh herbs and spices.

Skim milk, yogurt, ricotta, reduced- and lower-fat cheeses and spreads have all been used in the recipes to replace higher, full-fat equivalents. This substitution makes considerable fat and calorie savings. Occasionally a small amount of butter is used when the flavor is important to the dish, or perhaps Greek yogurt is recommended rather than a very low fat natural yogurt to add richness to the sauce, but overall there's a significant reduction in fat.

Similarly, hard cheeses such as parmesan and mature Cheddar are very high in fat, but they also have a wonderfully strong flavor, so that only a small amount is needed.

Robust ingredients such as fresh chilies, fresh root ginger, fresh garlic, citrus zests and juices, mustards, honey, vinegars, tomato paste pickles, chutneys and other condiments like soy and hoisin sauce can all be used to create exciting, flavorsome sauces.

Dried mushrooms and sun-dried tomatoes (not the varieties preserved in olive oil) are full of concentrated flavor and add a wonderful richness that really boosts any sauce they are added to.

The aromatic flavors of fresh herbs such as basil, bay leaves, cilantro, mint, oregano, parsley, rosemary, sage and thyme can all add their own individual fragrance to sauces, whether as classic partners or for experimenting with new and interesting combinations.

The Fat and Calorie Contents of Food

The following figures show the weight of fat (g) and the energy content of 100 g (3½ oz) of each food.

Dairy, Fats, Oils and Eggs	Fat (g)	Calories
Milk, whole	3.9	66
Milk, semi-skim	1.6	46
Milk, skim	0.1	33
Cream, heavy	48.0	449
Cream, light	19.1	198
Sour cream	19.9	205
Crème fraîche	40.0	380
Crème fraîche, half fat	15.0	169
Buttermilk	0.2	47
Cheddar cheese	34.4	412
Cheddar-type, reduced-fat	15.0	261
Parmesan cheese	32.7	452
Edam cheese	25.4	333
Full-fat soft cheese	31.0	313
Medium-fat (light) soft cheese, such as ricotta or curd	14.5	179
Quark	0.2	70
Cottage cheese, plain	3.9	98
Cottage cheese, reduced-fat	1.4	78
Low fat yogurt, plain	0.8	56
Greek-style yogurt	9.1	115
Mayonnaise	75.6	691
Mayonnaise, reduced-calorie	36.9	366
Butter	81.7	737
Margarine	81.6	739
Dairy/fat spread	73.4	662
Olive oil (reduced-fat) spread	60.0	544
Low fat spread	40.5	390
Very low fat spread	25.0	273
Corn, Sunflower, Safflower, Soya, Olive oils	99.9	899
Eggs (2 x size 4)	10.8	147
Egg yolk	30.5	339
Egg White	Trace	36

Information from The Composition of Foods, 5th Edition (1991) is reproduced with the permission of the Royal Society of Chemistry and the Controller of Her Majesty's Stationery Office.

Shopper's Guide to Fats and Spreads

Butter
Must contain at least 80% fat and all the fat must be natural milk fat (full cream). Can be used for spreading, broiling, roasting, shallow and stir-frying, sauces, baking, pastry-making and garnishing.

Margarine
Also must contain 80% fat, no more than 10% of which can be derived from milk. It has the same calorie value as butter. Also contains added vitamins A and D, which naturally occur in butter. Can be used either for spreading or cooking but doesn't have the same characteristic, creamy buttery flavor.

Polyunsaturated Margarine
Must contain at least 45% polyunsaturated fat but total fat and calorie content is the same as other margarines.

Dairy Spread
A blend of milk fats and vegetable oil. Brands vary in fat and calorie value but are generally slightly lower than butter and margarine. Has the convenience of a spread but can be used in cooking.

Olive Oil Spread
Reduced-fat spread with about 60% fat. It is made with olive oil so is high in monounsaturates and low in saturated fat (the type it's recommended to reduce). Suitable for spreading and stir-frying.

Reduced-Fat Spread
Based on vegetable oil or animal fats and generally about 60% fat, or ¾ that of butter or margarine. Can be used for spreading, baking, stir-frying at a gentle heat and in sauces.

Low Fat Spread/Half Fat Butter Spread
About half the fat (40% content) and calorie value of butter or margarine but with a high moisture content. Suitable for making all-in-one sauces (see below).

Very Low Fat Spread
Made from vegetable oils and various dairy ingredients. Only contains 25% fat, therefore very high moisture content and only suitable for spreading.

Three Healthy Ways to Make Low Fat Sauces

The traditional roux method for making a sauce won't work successfully if using a low fat spread. This is because of the high water content, which will evaporate on heating, leaving insufficient fat to blend with the flour. However, below are three quick and easy low fat alternatives.

1 The All-in-One Method: Place 2 tablespoons each of low fat spread and plain flour in a pan with 1 ¼ cups skim milk. Bring to a boil, stirring continuously until thickened and smooth. This method is perfect for making a milk-based sauce like cheese or parsley sauce.

2 Using Stock to Replace Fat: Sweat vegetables, such as onions, in a small amount of stock rather than frying in fat.

3 Using Cornstarch to Thicken: Rather than using the traditional roux method with fat and flour, blend 1 tablespoon cornstarch with 1–2 tablespoons cold water, then whisk into 1 ¼ cups simmering liquid, bring to a boil and cook for 1 minute, stirring continuously.

COOK'S TIP
Always cook all-in-one sauces over a low heat and whisk or stir constantly. If the sauce looks lumpy, remove from the heat and whisk thoroughly.

How to Adapt Classic Sauces

Mayonnaise
It isn't possible to make low fat mayonnaise at home, but you can buy commercially made reduced-calorie mayonnaise. To make further fat and calorie savings, substitute half the stated quantity with low fat natural yogurt or low fat ricotta cheese. This works well for mayonnaise-based dips or sauces like Thousand Island, which have tomato paste or ketchup added to the blended mayonnaise and low fat yogurt.

Hollandaise
This sauce is classically made with egg yolks, butter and vinegar. It's not worth making with margarine and it can't be made with low fat spreads. However, some fat saving can be made by using less butter and including buttermilk. Place 3 egg yolks in a bowl with the grated rind and 1 tablespoon juice from 1 lemon. Heat gently over a pan of water, stirring until thickened. Gradually whisk in 6 tablespoons softened butter, in small pieces, until smooth. Whisk in 3 tablespoons buttermilk and season. Reserve for special occasions.

Alternatively, flavor plain yogurt with a little French mustard and a little vinaigrette dressing and use to drizzle over asparagus.

Vinaigrette dressings
These are high in fat, even if you use monounsaturated oils, such as olive oil. You can buy reduced-calorie and oil-free dressings or, if you like the real thing, simply use less.

Fat Saving Tips for Making Sauces

• Use skim or semi-skim milk (if you find the former too thin and watery) in place of whole milk for white sauces.

• Use low fat natural yogurt or half fat crème fraîche in place of cream. If the yogurt or crème fraîche is to be heated, first stir in 2 table-spoons cornstarch to stabilize it and prevent the sauce from separating.

• Imitation creams, which are a blend of buttermilk and vegetable oils and which contain less fat than real cream, can be used as a lower-fat alternative in all sorts of sauces.

• Use a reduced-fat Cheddar-type cheese or a small amount of mature or vintage Cheddar or parmesan for maximum flavor.

• Substitute low fat ricotta or a skim milk soft cheese (such as quark or fromage blanc) in place of full-fat cream cheeses.

• Use a non-stick pan for cooking so less, if any, fat or oil is necessary.

Quick Low-Calorie, Oil-Free Dressings

Whisk together 6 tablespoons low fat natural yogurt, 2 tablespoons freshly squeezed lemon juice and season to taste with freshly ground black pepper.

If you prefer, wine, cider or fruit vinegar or even orange juice could be used in place of the lemon juice. Add freshly chopped herbs, crushed garlic, mustard, honey, grated horseradish or other flavorings, if you like.

Stocks

Many sauces depend for their depth and richness on a good quality stock base. Fresh stock will give the most balanced flavor and it is worth the effort to make it at home. It may be frozen successfully for several months. Canned beef bouillon and chicken broth are good substitutes. For everyday cooking, most cooks will use stock cubes, but these often have a salt base so taste carefully and season lightly.

FISH STOCK

INGREDIENTS
any fish bones, skin and
   trimmings available
1 onion
1 carrot
1 celery stalk
6 black peppercorns
2 bay leaves
3 stalks parsley

NUTRITIONAL NOTES
PER PORTION:

CALORIES 7 **FAT** 0.3 g
SATURATED FAT 0 **PROTEIN** 0.7 g
CARBOHYDRATE 0.6 g **FIBER** 0

1 Peel and coarsely slice the onion. Peel and chop the carrot, and scrub and slice the celery.

2 Place all the ingredients in a large saucepan and add enough water to cover. Bring to a boil, skim the surface and simmer uncovered for 20 minutes.

3 Strain and use immediately or store for two days in the refrigerator.

BROWN STOCK

INGREDIENTS
2 tbsp vegetable oil
3 lb shin, shank or neck of beef
   bones, cut into pieces
8 oz shin of beef, cut into pieces
bouquet garni
2 onions, trimmed and quartered
2 carrots, scrubbed and chopped
2 celery sticks, sliced
1 tsp black peppercorns
$^1/_2$ tsp salt

NUTRITIONAL NOTES
PER PORTION:

CALORIES 8 **FAT** 0.1 g
SATURATED FAT 0 **PROTEIN** 1.3 g
CARBOHYDRATE 0.4 g **FIBER** 0

1 Drizzle the vegetable oil over the bottom of a roasting pan, add the bones and meat. Coat in oil and bake at 425°F for 25–30 minutes or until well browned, turning regularly during cooking.

2 Transfer the meat and bones to a large saucepan, add the remaining ingredients and cover with 14 cups of water. Bring to the boil, skim the surface, then partially cover and simmer for 2½–3 hours or until reduced to 7 cups.

3 Strain the stock into a bowl. Cool and remove the solidified fat before use. Store for up to 4 days in the refrigerator.

CHICKEN OR WHITE STOCK

INGREDIENTS
1 onion
4 cloves
1 carrot
2 leeks
2 celery stalks
1 chicken carcass, cooked or raw,
   or 1½ lb veal bones cut into
   pieces
bouquet garni
8 black peppercorns
½ tsp salt

NUTRITIONAL NOTES
PER PORTION:

CALORIES 8 **FAT** 0.3 g
SATURATED FAT 0 **PROTEIN** 1.1 g
CARBOHYDRATE 0.3 g **FIBER** 0

1 Peel the onion, cut into quarters and spike each quarter with a clove. Scrub and coarsely chop the vegetables.

2 Break up the chicken carcass and place in a large saucepan with the remaining ingredients.

3 Cover with 7 cups water. Bring to a boil, skim the surface and simmer, partially covered, for 2 hours. Strain the stock into a bowl and allow to cool. When cold remove the hardened fat before using. Store for up to 4 days in the refrigerator.

VEGETABLE STOCK

INGREDIENTS
2 tbsp vegetable oil
1 onion
2 carrots
2 large celery stalks, plus any
   small amounts from the
   following: leeks, celery root,
   parsnip, turnip, cabbage or
   cauliflower trimmings,
   mushrooms peelings
bouquet garni
6 black peppercorns

NUTRITIONAL NOTES
PER PORTION:

CALORIES 7 **FAT** 0.3 g
SATURATED FAT 0 **PROTEIN** 0.3 g
CARBOHYDRATE 0.9 g **FIBER** 0

1 Peel, halve and slice the onion. Coarsely chop the remaining vegetables.

2 Heat the oil in a large pan and sauté the onion and vegetables until soft and lightly browned. Add the remaining ingredients and cover with 7 cups water.

3 Bring to a boil, skim the surface, then partially cover and simmer for 1½ hours. Strain the stock and allow to cool. Store in the refrigerator for 2–3 days.

Tomato and Dill Dip with Crunchy Baked Mushrooms

This creamy low fat dip is ideal to serve with crispy-coated bites as an informal appetizer.

NUTRITIONAL NOTES

PER SERVING:.

CALORIES 173 **PROTEIN** 11.88 g
FAT 6.04 g **SATURATED FAT** 3.24 g
CARBOHYDRATE 19.23 g **FIBER** 1.99 g
ADDED SUGAR 0 **SODIUM** 0.91 g

Serves 4–6

INGREDIENTS
2 cups fresh fine white bread crumbs
1½ tbsp finely grated sharp Cheddar cheese
1 tsp paprika
8 oz button mushrooms
2 egg whites

FOR THE TOMATO AND DILL DIP
4 ripe tomatoes
½ cup cottage cheese
4 tbsp natural low fat yogurt
1 garlic clove, crushed
2 tbsp chopped fresh dill
salt and freshly ground black pepper
sprig of fresh dill, to garnish

paprika

mushrooms

dill

tomatoes

bread crumbs

cottage cheese

1 Preheat the oven to 375°F. Mix together the bread crumbs, cheese and paprika in a bowl.

2 Wipe the mushrooms clean and trim the stems, if necessary. Lightly whisk the egg whites with a fork, until frothy.

3 Dip each mushroom into the egg whites, then into the bread crumb mixture. Repeat until all the mushrooms are coated.

4 Put the mushrooms on a non-stick baking sheet. Bake in the preheated oven for 15 minutes, or until tender and the coating has turned golden and crunchy.

5 Meanwhile, to make the dip, plunge the tomatoes into a saucepan of boiling water for 1 minute, then into a saucepan of cold water. Slip off the skins. Halve, remove the seeds and cores and roughly chop the flesh.

6 Put the cottage cheese, yogurt, garlic clove and dill into a mixing bowl and combine well. Season to taste. Stir in the chopped tomatoes. Spoon the mixture into a serving dish and garnish with a sprig of fresh dill. Serve the mushrooms hot, together with the dip.

Garlic and Chili Dip

Plainly cooked fish can sometimes be rather bland. This sauce will spice it up. Or try it with lightly battered, deep-fried vegetables.

Serves 4

INGREDIENTS
1 small red chili
1 in piece fresh ginger
2 garlic cloves
1 tsp mustard powder
1 tbsp chili sauce
2 tbsp olive oil
2 tbsp light soy sauce
juice of two limes
2 tbsp chopped fresh parsley
salt and pepper

mustard powder
parsley
red chili
ginger
light soy sauce
limes
chili sauce
garlic

1 Halve the chili, remove the seeds, stalk and membrane, and chop finely. Peel and coarsely chop the ginger.

2 Crush the chili, ginger, garlic and mustard powder to a paste, using a pestle and mortar.

3 In a bowl, mix together all the remaining ingredients, except the parsley. Add the paste and blend it in. Cover and chill for 24 hours.

4 Stir in the parsley and season to taste. It is best to serve in small individual bowls for dipping.

COOK'S TIP

Large shrimps are ideal served with this sauce. Remove the shell but leave the tails intact so there is something to hold on to for dipping.

NUTRITIONAL NOTES
PER PORTION:

CALORIES 41 **FAT** 3.3 g
SATURATED FAT 0.4 g **PROTEIN** 1.2 g
CARBOHYDRATE 1.8 g **FIBER** 0.4 g

Asian Hoisin Dip

This speedy Asian dip needs no cooking and can be made in just a few minutes – it tastes great with mini spring rolls or shrimp crackers.

Serves 4

INGREDIENTS
4 scallions
1½-in piece ginger
2 red chilies
2 garlic cloves
¼ cup hoisin sauce
½ cup passata
1 tsp sesame oil (optional)

scallions

ginger

garlic

sesame oil

red chilies

hoisin sauce

passata

1 Trim off and discard the green ends of the scallions. Slice the remainder very thinly.

2 Peel the ginger with a swivel-bladed vegetable peeler, then chop it finely.

3 Halve the chilies lengthwise and remove their seeds. Finely slice the flesh horizontally into tiny strips. Finely chop the garlic.

4 Stir together the hoisin sauce, passata, scallions, ginger, chili, garlic and sesame oil, if using, and serve within 1 hour.

COOK'S TIP

Hoisin sauce makes an excellent base for full-flavor dips, especially when combining crunchy vegetables and other Asian seasonings.

NUTRITIONAL NOTES
PER PORTION:

CALORIES 33 **FAT** 0.9 g
SATURATED FAT 0.1 g **PROTEIN** 1.3 g
CARBOHYDRATE 5.3 g **FIBER** 0.4 g

Tsatziki

Serve this classic Greek dip with strips of toasted pita bread.

Serves 4

INGREDIENTS
1 small cucumber
4 scallions
1 garlic clove
scant 1 cup plain
   yogurt
3 tbsp chopped fresh mint
fresh mint sprig, to garnish (optional)
salt and pepper

small
cucumber

scallions

garlic

plain
yogurt

mint

COOK'S TIP

Choose Greek-style yogurt for this dip – it has a higher fat content than most yogurts, but this gives it a deliciously rich, creamy texture.

I Trim the ends from the cucumber, then cut it into ¼-in dice.

2 Trim the scallions and garlic, then chop both very finely.

NUTRITIONAL NOTES
PER PORTION:

CALORIES 65 FAT 4.7 g
SATURATED FAT 2.9 g PROTEIN 3.9 g
CARBOHYDRATE 2.1 g FIBER 0.3 g

3 Beat the yogurt until smooth, if necessary, then gently stir in the cucumber, onions, garlic and mint.

4 Transfer the mixture to a serving bowl and add salt and plenty of freshly ground black pepper to taste. Chill until ready to serve and then garnish with a small mint sprig, if desired.

Fat-free Saffron Dip

Serve this mild dip with fresh vegetable crudités –
it is particularly good with cauliflower florets.

Serves 4

INGREDIENTS
1 tbsp boiling water
small pinch of saffron strands
scant 1 cup fat-free
    cottage cheese
10 fresh chives
10 fresh basil leaves
salt and pepper

*saffron
strands*

*cottage
cheese*

basil leaves

chives

1 Pour the boiling water into a small container and add the saffron strands. Set aside to infuse for 3 minutes.

2 Beat the cottage cheese until smooth, then stir in the infused saffron liquid.

VARIATION
Leave out the saffron and add a squeeze of lemon or lime juice instead.

NUTRITIONAL NOTES
PER PORTION:

CALORIES 29 **FAT** 0.1 g
SATURATED FAT 0.1 g **PROTEIN** 3.9 g
CARBOHYDRATE 3.5 g **FIBER** 0

3 Use a pair of scissors to snip the chives into the dip. Tear the basil leaves into small pieces and stir them in.

4 Add salt and pepper to taste. Serve immediately.

Watercress and Arugula Sauce with Parsnip Gougères

Nutty puffs with a sweet parsnip center are the perfect accompaniment to this sauce.

Makes 18 (Serves 6)

INGREDIENTS
½ cup butter
1¼ cups water
¼ cup all-purpose flour
½ cup whole wheat flour
3 eggs, beaten
1 oz reduced-fat Cheddar
  cheese, grated
pinch of cayenne pepper or paprika
⅔ cup pecans, chopped
1 medium parsnip, cut into ¾ in pieces
1 tbsp skim milk
2 tsp sesame seeds

FOR THE SAUCE
5 oz watercress, trimmed
5 oz arugula, trimmed
¾ cup low fat yogurt
salt, grated nutmeg and freshly ground
  black pepper
watercress sprigs, to garnish

1 Preheat the oven to 400°F. Place the butter and water in a pot. Bring to a boil and add all the flour at once. Beat vigorously until the mixture leaves the sides of the pan and forms a ball. Remove from heat and allow the mixture to cool slightly. Beat in the eggs a little at a time until the mixture is shiny and soft enough to fall gently from a spoon.

2 Beat in the Cheddar, cayenne pepper or paprika and the chopped pecans.

3 Lightly grease a cookie sheet and drop onto it 18 heaped tablespoons of the mixture. Place a piece of parsnip on each and top with another heaped tablespoon of the mixture.

4 Brush the puffs with a little milk and sprinkle with sesame seeds. Bake in the oven for 25–30 minutes until golden.

pecans *parsnips*
Cheddar
arugula
wholewheat flour
plain flour *egg* *yogurt* *watercress*

NUTRITIONAL NOTES

PER PORTION:

CALORIES 83 **FAT** 6.1 g
SATURATED FAT 2.8 g **PROTEIN** 2.6 g
CARBOHYDRATE 4.9 g **FIBER** 0.7 g

5 Meanwhile make the sauce. Bring a pan of water to a boil and blanch the watercress and arugula for 2–3 minutes. Drain and immediately refresh in cold water. Drain well and chop.

6 Purée the watercress and arugula in a blender or food processor with the yogurt until smooth. Season to taste with salt, nutmeg and freshly ground black pepper. To reheat, place the sauce in a bowl over a gently simmering pot of hot water and heat gently, taking care not to let the sauce curdle. Garnish with watercress.

Creamy Raspberry Dressing with Asparagus

Raspberry vinegar gives this quick low fat dressing a refreshing, tangy flavor – the perfect accompaniment to asparagus.

Serves 4

INGREDIENTS
1½ pounds thin asparagus spears
2 tablespoons raspberry vinegar
½ teaspoon salt
1 teaspoon Dijon-style mustard
4 tablespoons half fat crème fraîche
  or natural low fat yogurt
ground white pepper
4 ounces fresh raspberries

asparagus spears

raspberry vinegar

Dijon-style mustard

half fat crème fraîche

fresh raspberries

NUTRITIONAL NOTES
PER PORTION:

CALORIES 60 **FAT** 1.3 g
SATURATED FAT 0.1 g **PROTEIN** 6.2 g
CARBOHYDRATE 6.0 g **FIBER** 3.6 g

1 Fill a large wide frying pan, or wok, with water about 4 inches deep and bring to a boil.

2 Trim the tough ends of the asparagus spears. If desired, remove the "scales" using a vegetable peeler.

3 Tie the asparagus spears into two bundles. Lower the bundles into the boiling water and cook for 3–5 minutes, or until just tender.

4 Carefully remove the asparagus bundles from the boiling water using a slotted spoon and immerse them in cold water to stop the cooking. Drain and untie the bundles. Pat dry with paper towels. Chill the asparagus for at least 1 hour.

5 Mix together the vinegar and salt in a bowl and stir with a fork until dissolved. Stir in the mustard. Gradually stir in the crème fraîche or yogurt until blended. Add pepper to taste. To serve, place the asparagus on individual plates and drizzle the dressing across the middle of the spears. Garnish with the fresh raspberries and serve at once.

Egg and Lemon Sauce with Leeks

This sauce has a delicious tangy taste and brings out the best in fresh leeks.

Serves 4

INGREDIENTS
1½ pounds baby leeks
1 tablespoon cornstarch
2 teaspoons sugar
1 egg yolk
juice of 1½ lemons
salt

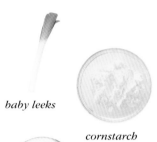

baby leeks

cornstarch

sugar   *egg*

lemons

1 Trim the leeks, slit them from top to bottom and rinse very well under cold water to remove any dirt.

2 Place the leeks in a large saucepan so they lie flat on the base, cover with water and add a little salt. Bring to a boil, cover and gently simmer for 4–5 minutes until just tender.

3 Carefully remove the leeks using a slotted spoon, drain well and arrange in a shallow serving dish. Reserve a scant 1 cup of the cooking liquid.

4 Blend the cornstarch with the cooled cooking liquid and place in a small saucepan. Bring to a boil, stirring all the time, and cook over low heat until the sauce thickens slightly. Stir in the sugar and then remove the saucepan from the heat and allow to cool slightly.

5 Beat the egg yolk thoroughly with the lemon juice and stir gradually into the cooled sauce. Cook over low heat, stirring all the time, until the sauce is fairly thick. Be careful not to overheat the sauce or it may curdle. As soon as the sauce has thickened remove the pan from the heat and continue stirring for a minute. Taste and add salt or sugar as necessary. Cool slightly.

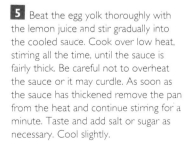

6 Stir the cooled sauce with a wooden spoon. Pour the sauce over the leeks and then cover and chill well for at least 2 hours before serving.

Spicy Cocktail Dressing with Crab and Pasta Salad

Serves 6

INGREDIENTS
12 ounces fusilli
1 small red bell pepper, seeded and
   finely chopped
2 x 6-ounce cans white crab
   meat, drained
4 ounces cherry tomatoes, halved
¼ cucumber, halved, seeded and
   sliced into crescents
1 tablespoon lemon juice
1¼ cups low-fat yogurt
2 sticks celery, finely chopped
2 teaspoons horseradish cream
½ teaspoon ground paprika
½ teaspoon Dijon mustard
2 tablespoons salsa
salt and ground black pepper
fresh basil, to garnish

celery

paprika

lemon

red pepper *fusilli*

cucumber

crab meat

cherry tomatoes

low-fat yogurt

salsa *horseradish cream*

1 Cook the pasta in a large pan of boiling, salted water according to the instructions on the package. Drain and rinse thoroughly under cold water.

2 Cover the chopped red bell pepper with boiling water and let stand for 1 minute. Drain and rinse under cold water. Pat dry with paper towels.

NUTRITIONAL NOTES

PER PORTION:

ENERGY 305 calories **FAT** 2.5g
SATURATED FAT 0.5g **CHOLESTEROL** 43mg
CARBOHYDRATE 53g **FIBER** 2.9g

3 Drain the crab meat and pick over carefully for pieces of shell. Put into a bowl with the halved tomatoes and sliced cucumber. Season with salt and pepper and sprinkle with lemon juice.

4 To make the dressing, add the red pepper to the yogurt, celery, horseradish, paprika, mustard and salsa. Mix the pasta with the dressing and transfer to a serving dish. Spoon the crab mixture on top and garnish with fresh basil.

Egg and Lemon Mayonnaise

This recipe draws on the contrasting flavors of egg and lemon, with the chopped parsley providing a fresh finish – perfect for potato salad. Serve with an assortment of cold meats or fish for a simple, tasty meal.

Serves 4

INGREDIENTS
2 lb new potatoes, scrubbed
  or scraped
1 medium onion, finely chopped
1 egg, hard-boiled
⅔ cup reduced-calorie
  mayonnaise
1 garlic clove, crushed
finely grated zest and juice of 1 lemon
4 tbsp chopped fresh parsley
salt and pepper

COOK'S TIP

At certain times of the year potatoes are inclined to fall apart when boiled. This usually coincides with the end of a particular season when potatoes become starchy. Early-season varieties are therefore best for making salads.

egg

garlic

onion

lemon

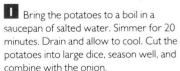

new potatoes

1 Bring the potatoes to a boil in a saucepan of salted water. Simmer for 20 minutes. Drain and allow to cool. Cut the potatoes into large dice, season well, and combine with the onion.

2 Shell the hard-cooked egg and grate into a mixing bowl, then add the mayonnaise. Combine the garlic and lemon zest and juice in a small bowl and stir into the mayonnaise.

3 Fold in the chopped parsley, mix thoroughly into the potatoes, and serve.

NUTRITIONAL NOTES

PER PORTION:

CALORIES 303 **FAT** 12.9 g
SATURATED FAT 2.1 g **PROTEIN** 6.7 g
CARBOHYDRATE 42.4 g **FIBER** 3.2 g

Citrus Sauce with Baby Zucchini

If baby zucchini are unavailable, you can use larger ones, but they should be cooked whole.

Serves 4

INGREDIENTS
12 oz baby zucchini
4 scallions, finely sliced
1 in fresh ginger root, grated
2 tbsp cider vinegar
1 tbsp light soy sauce
1 tsp soft light brown sugar
3 tbsp vegetable stock
finely grated rind and juice of ½
   lemon and ½ orange
1 tsp cornstarch

orange

lemon

zucchini

ginger

scallions

NUTRITIONAL NOTES
PER SERVING:

CALORIES 33 PROTEIN 2.18 g
FAT 0.42 g SATURATED FAT 0.09 g
CARBOHYDRATE 5.33 g FIBER 0.92 g
ADDED SUGAR 1.31 g SODIUM 0.55 g

1 Cook the zucchini in lightly salted boiling water for 3-4 minutes, or until just tender. Drain well.

2 Meanwhile put all the remaining ingredients, except the cornstarch, into a small saucepan and bring to a boil. Simmer for 3 minutes.

3 Blend the cornstarch with 2 tsp of cold water and add to the sauce. Bring to a boil, stirring continuously, until the sauce has thickened.

4 Pour the sauce over the zucchini and gently heat, shaking the pan to coat evenly. Transfer to a warmed serving dish and serve.

Rich Tomato Sauce

For a full tomato flavor and rich red color use only really ripe tomatoes. Fresh plum tomatoes are an excellent choice if you can find them.

Serves 4-6

INGREDIENTS
2 tbsp olive oil
1 large onion, chopped
2 garlic cloves, crushed
1 carrot, finely chopped
1 celery stalk, finely chopped
1 1/2 lb tomatoes, peeled and
   chopped
2/3 cup red wine
2/3 cup vegetable stock
1 bouquet garni
1 tbsp tomato paste
1/2–1 tsp sugar
salt and pepper

vegetable stock
onion
carrot
red wine
olive oil
garlic
tomato paste
tomatoes
celery
bouquet garni

1 Heat the oil and sauté the onion and garlic until soft. Add the carrot and celery and continue to cook, stirring occasionally, until golden.

2 Stir in the tomatoes, wine, stock, bouquet garni and seasoning. Bring to a boil, cover and simmer for 45 minutes, stirring occasionally.

NUTRITIONAL NOTES
PER PORTION:

CALORIES 134 **FAT** 6.2 g
SATURATED FAT 0.8 g **PROTEIN** 2.4 g
CARBOHYDRATE 11.9 g **FIBER** 3.0 g

3 Remove the bouquet garni and adjust the seasoning, adding sugar and tomato paste as necessary.

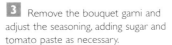

4 Serve the sauce as it is or, for a smoother texture, purée in a blender or food processor, or press through a strainer. Spoon over sliced succhini or whole fava beans.

Mushroom Sauce with Carrot Mousse

Combining this tasty sauce with an impressive, yet easy-to-make, mousse makes healthy eating a pleasure.

NUTRITIONAL NOTES

Per serving:

Calories 174 **Protein** 12.65 g
Fat 5.90 g **Saturated Fat** 1.44 g
Carbohydrate 18.69 g **Fiber** 3.13 g
Added Sugar 0 **Sodium** 0.42 g

Serves 4

INGREDIENTS

12 oz carrots, roughly chopped
1 small red bell pepper, seeded and
    roughly chopped
3 tbsp vegetable stock or water
2 eggs
1 egg white
1/2 cup quark or low fat cream cheese
1 tbsp chopped fresh tarragon
salt and freshly ground black pepper
sprig of fresh tarragon, to garnish
boiled rice and leeks, to serve

FOR THE MUSHROOM SAUCE

2 tbsp low fat spread
6 oz mushrooms, sliced
2 tbsp flour
1 cup skim milk

carrots
egg white
mushrooms
pepper
eggs
flour
cream cheese
low fat spread

1 Preheat the oven to 375°F. Line the bases of four 2/3 cup ramekin dishes with non-stick baking paper. Put the carrots and red pepper in a small saucepan with the vegetable stock or water. Cover and cook for 5 minutes, or until tender. Drain well.

2 Lightly beat the eggs and egg white together. Mix with the quark or low fat cream cheese. Season to taste. Purée the cooked vegetables in a food processor or blender. Add the cheese mixture and process for a few seconds more until smooth. Stir in the chopped tarragon.

3 Divide the carrot mixture between the prepared ramekin dishes and cover with foil. Place the dishes in a roasting pan half-filled with hot water. Bake in the oven for 35 minutes, or until set.

4 For the mushroom sauce, melt 1 tbsp of the low fat spread in a frying pan. Add the mushrooms and gently sauté for 5 minutes, until soft.

5 Put the remaining low fat spread in a small saucepan together with the flour and milk. Cook over medium heat, stirring all the time, until the sauce thickens. Stir in the mushrooms and season to taste.

6 Turn out each mousse onto a serving plate. Spoon over a little sauce and serve the remainder separately. Garnish with a sprig of fresh tarragon and serve with boiled rice and leeks.

Quick Tomato Sauce with Fish Balls

This quick sauce is ideal to serve with fish balls and makes a good choice for children. If you like, add a dash of chili sauce.

Serves 4

INGREDIENTS
1 pound white fish fillets, skinned
4 tablespoons fresh wholewheat
  bread crumbs
2 tablespoons snipped chives
  or scallions
14-ounce can chopped tomatoes
¾ cup button mushrooms, sliced
salt and pepper

white fish fillets

fresh wholewheat bread crumbs

scallions

chopped tomatoes

button mushrooms

1 Cut the fish fillets into large chunks and place in a food processor. Add the wholewheat bread crumbs and chives or scallions. Season to taste with salt and pepper and process until the fish is finely chopped but still has some texture left.

2 Divide the fish mixture into about 16 even-size pieces, then mold them into balls with your hands.

3 Place the tomatoes and mushrooms in a wide saucepan and cook over medium heat until boiling. Add the fish balls, cover and simmer for about 10 minutes, until cooked. Serve hot.

COOK'S TIP
Cod is a good choice for this dish but if it's not available, use flounder or sole instead.

NUTRITIONAL NOTES
PER PORTION:

CALORIES 137 **FAT** 1.4 g
SATURATED FAT 0.2 g **PROTEIN** 22.3 g
CARBOHYDRATE 9.4 g **FIBER** 1.8 g

Warm Green Tartare Sauce with Seafood

Serves 4

INGREDIENTS

½ cup low-fat sour cream
2 teaspoons coarse-grained mustard
2 garlic cloves, crushed
2–3 tablespoons fresh lime juice
4 tablespoons chopped fresh parsley
2 tablespoons snipped chives
12 ounces black tagliatelle
12 large scallops
4 tablespoons white wine
⅔ cup fish stock
salt and ground black pepper
lime wedges and parsley sprigs,
    to garnish

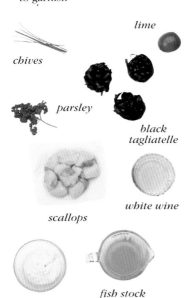

lime

chives

parsley

black
tagliatelle

scallops

white wine

fish stock

low-fat sour
cream

garlic

1 To make the tartare sauce, mix the sour cream, mustard, garlic, lime juice, herbs and seasoning together in a bowl.

2 Cook the pasta in a large pan of boiling, salted water until *al dente*. Drain thoroughly.

NUTRITIONAL NOTES
PER PORTION:

ENERGY 433 calories **FAT** 3.4g
SATURATED FAT 0.6g **CHOLESTEROL** 45mg
CARBOHYDRATE 68g **FIBER** 3.4g

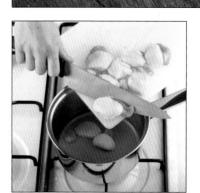

3 Slice the scallops in half, horizontally. Put the white wine and fish stock into a saucepan. Heat to simmering point. Add the scallops and cook very gently for 3–4 minutes (no longer or they will become tough).

4 Remove the scallops. Boil the wine and stock to reduce by half and add the green sauce to the pan. Heat gently to warm, replace the scallops and cook for 1 minute. Spoon over the pasta and garnish with lime wedges and parsley.

Lemon and Chive Sauce with Herbed Fish Cakes

This tangy sauce makes a delicious accompaniment to fish cakes.

Serves 4

INGREDIENTS
12 oz potatoes, peeled
5 tbsp skimmed milk
12 oz haddock or flounder fillets,
    skinned
1 tbsp lemon juice
1 tbsp creamed horseradish
2 tbsp chopped fresh Italian
    parsley
flour, for dusting
2 cups fresh whole wheat
    bread crumbs
salt and freshly ground black pepper
sprig of Italian parsley, to garnish
snow peas and a sliced tomato and
    onion salad, to serve

FOR THE LEMON AND CHIVE SAUCE
thinly pared rind and juice of
    ½ small lemon
½ cup dry white wine
2 thin slices fresh ginger root
2 tsp cornstarch
2 tbsp snipped fresh chives

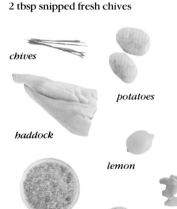

chives

potatoes

haddock

lemon

ginger

bread crumbs

parsley

1 Cook the potatoes in a large saucepan of boiling water for 15-20 minutes. Drain and mash with the milk and season to taste.

2 Purée the fish together with the lemon juice and horseradish in a blender or food processor. Mix together with the potatoes and parsley.

3 With floured hands, shape the mixture into eight fish cakes and coat with the bread crumbs. Chill in the refrigerator for 30 minutes.

4 Cook the fish cakes under a pre-heated moderate broiler for 5 minutes on each side, until browned.

5 To make the sauce, cut the lemon rind into julienne strips and put into a large saucepan together with the lemon juice, wine and ginger and season to taste.

NUTRITIONAL NOTES

PER SERVING:

CALORIES 232 **PROTEIN** 19.99 g
FAT 1.99 g **SATURATED FAT** 0.26 g
CARBOHYDRATE 30.62 g **FIBER** 3.11 g
ADDED SUGAR 0 **SODIUM** 0.82 g

6 Simmer uncovered for 6 minutes. Blend the cornstarch with 1 tbsp of cold water. Add to the saucepan and simmer until clear. Stir in the chives immediately before serving. Serve the sauce hot with the fish cakes, garnished with sprigs of Italian parsley and accompanied with snow peas and a sliced tomato and onion salad.

Parsley Sauce with Smoked Haddock and Pasta

Serves 4

INGREDIENTS

1 pound smoked haddock fillet
1 small leek or onion, sliced thickly
1¼ cups skim milk
a bouquet garni (bay leaf, thyme and parsley)
1 ounce low-fat margarine
1 ounce flour
2 tablespoons chopped fresh parsley
8 ounces pasta shells
salt and ground black pepper
½ ounce toasted slivered almonds, to serve

leek *salt*

haddock fillet

parsley

bay leaves

pepper

pasta shells

skim milk

flour *low-fat margarine*

1 Remove all the skin and any bones from the haddock. Put into a pan with the leek or onion, milk and bouquet garni. Bring to a boil, cover and simmer gently for about 8–10 minutes until the fish flakes easily.

2 Strain, reserving the milk for making the sauce, and discard the bouquet garni.

NUTRITIONAL NOTES
PER PORTION:

ENERGY 405 calories **FAT** 6.9g
SATURATED FAT 1.0g **CHOLESTEROL** 42mg
CARBOHYDRATE 58g **FIBER** 3.7g

3 Put the margarine, flour and reserved milk into a pan. Bring to a boil and whisk until smooth. Season and add the fish and leek or onion.

4 Cook the pasta in a large pan of boiling water until *al dente*. Drain thoroughly and stir into the sauce with the chopped parsley. Serve immediately, scattered with almonds.

Sorrel Sauce with Salmon Steaks

The sharp flavor of the sorrel sauce balances the richness of the fish. If sorrel is not available, use finely chopped watercress instead.

Serves 2

INGREDIENTS

2 salmon steaks (about
  9 ounces each)
1 teaspoon olive oil
1 tablespoon butter
2 shallots, finely chopped
3 tablespoons half fat crème fraîche
3½ ounces fresh sorrel leaves,
  washed and patted dry
salt and pepper
fresh sage, to garnish

salmon

olive oil

shallots

butter

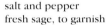

half fat crème fraîche

sorrel leaves

sage

1 Season the salmon steaks with salt and pepper. Brush a nonstick frying pan with the oil.

2 In a small saucepan, melt the butter over medium heat. Add the shallots and fry for 2–3 minutes, stirring frequently, until just softened.

3 Add the crème fraîche and the sorrel to the shallots and cook until the sorrel is completely wilted, stirring constantly.

4 Meanwhile, place the frying pan over medium heat until hot.

COOK'S TIP

If preferred, cook the salmon steaks in a microwave oven for about 4–5 minutes, tightly covered, or according to the manufacturer's guidelines.

5 Add the salmon steaks and cook for about 5 minutes, turning once, until the flesh is opaque next to the bone. If you're not sure, pierce with the tip of a sharp knife; the juices should run clear.

6 Arrange the salmon steaks on two warmed plates, garnish with sage and serve with the sorrel sauce.

NUTRITIONAL NOTES

PER PORTION:

CALORIES 86 **FAT** 6.8 g
SATURATED FAT 3.9 g **PROTEIN** 3.7 g
CARBOHYDRATE 2.8 g **FIBER** 1.0 g

Mexican Barbecue Sauce

This spicy, tomato and mustard sauce is delicious served with char-grilled salmon fillets – cook them either on a barbecue or under a hot broiler.

NUTRITIONAL NOTES
PER PORTION:

CALORIES 125 **FAT** 3.5 g
SATURATED FAT 1.4 g **PROTEIN** 2.8 g
CARBOHYDRATE 21.9 g **FIBER** 1.6 g

Serves 4

INGREDIENTS
1 small red onion
1 garlic clove
6 plum tomatoes
2 tsp butter
3 tbsp tomato ketchup
2 tbsp Dijon mustard
2 tbsp dark brown sugar
1 tbsp honey
1 tsp ground cayenne pepper
1 tbsp ancho chili powder
1 tbsp ground paprika
1 tbsp Worcestershire sauce
4 x 6 oz salmon fillets

cayenne pepper

Dijon mustard

dark brown sugar

plum tomato

salmon fillet

red onion

tomato ketchup

1 Finely chop the red onion and finely dice the garlic.

2 Dice the tomatoes.

3 Melt the butter in a large, heavy-based saucepan and gently cook the onion and garlic until translucent.

4 Add the tomatoes and simmer for 15 minutes.

5 Add the remaining ingredients except the salmon and simmer for a further 20 minutes. Process the mixture in a food processor fitted with a metal blade and leave to cool.

6 Brush the salmon with the sauce and chill for at least 2 hours. Barbecue or broil for about 2–3 minutes either side, brushing on the sauce when necessary.

Cranberry Sauce

This is the sauce for roast turkey, but don't just keep it for festive occasions. The vibrant color and tart taste are a perfect partner to any white roast meat, and it makes a great addition to a chicken sandwich.

Serves 6

INGREDIENTS
1 orange
8 oz cranberries
1¼ cups sugar

orange

sugar

cranberries

NUTRITIONAL NOTES
PER PORTION:

CALORIES 163 **FAT** 0.1 g
SATURATED FAT 0 **PROTEIN** 0.4 g
CARBOHYDRATE 42.9 g **FIBER** 1.6 g

1 Pare the rind thinly from the orange, taking care not to remove any white pith. Squeeze the juice.

2 Place in a saucepan with the cranberries, sugar and ⅔ cup water.

3 Bring to a boil, stirring until the sugar has dissolved, then simmer for 10–15 minutes or until the berries burst.

4 Remove the rind and allow to cool before serving.

Mint Sauce

Tart, yet sweet, this simple sauce is the perfect foil to rich meat. It's best served, of course, with new season's roast lamb, but is wonderful, too, with grilled lamb chops or pan-fried duck.

Serves 6

INGREDIENTS
small bunch mint
1 tbsp sugar
2 tbsp boiling water
3 tbsp white wine vinegar

white wine vinegar

mint

sugar

NUTRITIONAL NOTES
PER PORTION:

CALORIES 12 **FAT** 0.1 g
SATURATED FAT 0 **PROTEIN** 0.2 g
CARBOHYDRATE 2.9 g **FIBER** 0

1 Strip the leaves from the stalks.

2 Chop the leaves very finely.

3 Place in a bowl with the sugar and pour on the boiling water. Stir well and let stand for 5–10 minutes.

4 Add the vinegar and let stand for 1–2 hours before serving.

Barbecue Sauce

Brush this sauce liberally over chicken drumsticks, chops or kebabs before cooking on the barbecue, or serve as a hot or cold accompaniment to hot dogs and burgers.

Serves 4

INGREDIENTS
2 tsp vegetable oil
1 large onion, chopped
2 garlic cloves, crushed
14 oz can tomatoes
2 tbsp Worcestershire
   sauce
1 tbsp white wine vinegar
3 tbsp honey
1 tsp mustard powder
½ tsp chili seasoning or
   mild chili powder
salt and pepper

honey

white wine vinegar

onion

vegetable oil

tomatoes

garlic

mild chili powder

mustard powder

Worcestershire sauce

1 Heat the oil and fry the onions and garlic until soft.

2 Stir in the remaining ingredients and simmer, uncovered, for 15–20 minutes, stirring occasionally. Cool slightly.

NUTRITIONAL NOTES
PER PORTION:
CALORIES 102 **FAT** 2.1 g
SATURATED FAT 0.2 g **PROTEIN** 2.8 g
CARBOHYDRATE 19.3 g **FIBER** 1.4 g

3 Pour into a food processor or blender and process until smooth.

4 Press through a strainer if you prefer and adjust the seasoning.

Yellow Bell Pepper Sauce

Yellow bell peppers make a colorful low fat sauce to serve with stuffed turkey escalopes.

Serves 4

INGREDIENTS
2 teaspoons olive oil
2 large yellow bell peppers, seeded
  and chopped
1 small onion, chopped
1 tablespoon freshly squeezed
  orange juice
1¼ cups chicken broth
4 turkey scallops
3 ounces reduced-fat soft cheese
12 fresh basil leaves
salt and pepper

olive oil

yellow bell peppers

orange

onion

chicken broth

turkey

low fat soft cheese

basil leaves

1 To make yellow bell pepper sauce, heat half the oil in a pan and gently fry the bell peppers and onion until beginning to soften. Add the orange juice and broth and cook until very soft.

2 Meanwhile, lay the turkey scallops out flat and beat them out lightly. Spread the turkey scallops with the reduced-fat soft cheese. Chop half the basil and sprinkle on top, then roll up, tucking in the ends like an envelope, and secure neatly with half a cocktail stick.

3 Heat the remaining oil in a frying pan and fry the scallops for 7–8 minutes, turning them frequently, until golden brown and cooked.

4 While the scallops are cooking, press the bell pepper mixture through a strainer or blend until smooth, then strain back into the pan. Season to taste and warm through, or serve cold, with the scallops garnished with the remaining basil leaves.

COOK'S TIP

Chicken breast fillets or veal scallops could be used in place of the turkey.

NUTRITIONAL NOTES

PER PORTION:

CALORIES 186 **FAT** 3.1 g
SATURATED FAT 0.7 g **PROTEIN** 33.2 g
CARBOHYDRATE 6.6 g **FIBER** 1.5 g

Herbed Yogurt Dressing

Serves 6

INGREDIENTS
1 pound beef fillet
1 pound fresh tagliatelle with
    sun-dried tomatoes and herbs
4 ounces cherry tomatoes
¹/₂ cucumber

FOR THE MARINADE
1 tablespoon soy sauce
1 tablespoon sherry
1 tablespoon fresh ginger, grated
1 garlic clove, crushed

FOR THE HERB DRESSING
2–3 tablespoons horseradish
²/₃ cup low-fat yogurt
1 garlic clove, crushed
2–3 tablespoons chopped fresh
    herbs (chives, parsley, thyme)
salt and ground black pepper

cherry
tomatoes

cucumber

fillet beef

fresh ginger

garlic

tagliatelle

thyme

low-fat
yogurt

horseradish
sauce

parsley

soy sauce

chives

1 Mix all the marinade ingredients together in a shallow dish, put the beef in and turn it over to coat it. Cover with plastic wrap and leave for 30 minutes to allow the flavors to penetrate the meat.

2 Preheat the grill. Lift the fillet out of the marinade and pat it dry with paper towels. Place on a broiler rack and broil for 8 minutes on each side, basting with the marinade during cooking.

3 Transfer to a plate, cover with foil and leave to stand for 20 minutes.

4 Put all the dressing ingredients into a bowl and mix together thoroughly. Cook the pasta according to the directions on the package, drain thoroughly, rinse under cold water and leave to dry.

5 Cut the cherry tomatoes in half. Cut the cucumber in half lengthways, scoop out the seeds with a teaspoon and slice thinly into crescents.

6 Put the pasta, cherry tomatoes, cucumber and dressing into a bowl and toss to coat. Slice the beef thinly and arrange on a plate with the pasta salad.

NUTRITIONAL NOTES
PER PORTION:

ENERGY 374 calories **FAT** 5.7g
SATURATED FAT 1.7g **CHOLESTEROL** 46mg
CARBOHYDRATE 57g **FIBER** 2.9g

Tomato and Rice Sauce with Turkey Meatballs

Meatballs simmered with rice in a tomato sauce.

COOK'S TIP

To make carrot and zucchini ribbons, cut the vegetables lengthwise into thin strips using a vegetable peeler, and blanch or steam until cooked through.

NUTRITIONAL NOTES

PER SERVING:

CALORIES 190 **PROTEIN** 18.04 g
FAT 1.88 g **SATURATED FAT** 0.24 g
CARBOHYDRATE 26.96 g **FIBER** 1.04 g
ADDED SUGAR 0 **SODIUM** 0.32 g

Serves 4

INGREDIENTS
1 oz white bread, crusts removed
2 tbsp skim milk
1 garlic clove, crushed
½ tsp caraway seeds
8 oz ground turkey
1 egg white
1½ cups fresh or canned low salt chicken stock
14 oz can plum tomatoes
1 tbsp tomato paste
½ cup rice
salt and freshly ground black pepper
1 tbsp chopped fresh basil, to garnish
carrot and zucchini ribbons, to serve

basil

ground turkey

rice

bread

tomato paste

plum tomatoes

caraway seeds

garlic

1 Cut the bread into small cubes and put into a mixing bowl. Sprinkle over the milk and leave to soak for 5 minutes.

2 Add the garlic clove, caraway seeds, turkey, salt and freshly ground black pepper to the bread. Mix together well.

3 Whisk the egg white until stiff, then fold, half at a time, into the turkey mixture. Chill for 10 minutes in the refrigerator.

4 Put the stock, tomatoes and tomato paste into a large, heavy-based saucepan and bring to a boil.

5 Add the rice, stir and cook briskly for about 5 minutes. Turn the heat down to a gentle simmer.

6 Meanwhile, shape the turkey mixture into 16 small balls. Carefully drop them into the tomato stock and simmer for a further 8-10 minutes, or until the turkey balls and rice are cooked. Garnish with chopped basil, and serve with carrot and zucchini ribbons.

Creamy Orange Sauce with Chicken

This sauce is deceptively creamy – in fact it is made with low fat ricotta cheese which is virtually fat-free. The brandy adds a richer flavor, but is optional.

Serves 4

INGREDIENTS
8 chicken drumsticks or
  thighs, skinned
3 tablespoons brandy
1¼ cups orange juice
3 scallions, chopped
2 teaspoons cornstarch
6 tablespoons low fat ricotta cheese
salt and pepper

chicken

brandy

oranges

scallions

cornstarch

low fat ricotta cheese

NUTRITIONAL NOTES
PER PORTION:

CALORIES 224 **FAT** 6.7 g
SATURATED FAT 2.2 g **PROTEIN** 25.2 g
CARBOHYDRATE 10.1 g **FIBER** 0.2 g

1 Fry the chicken pieces without fat in a nonstick or heavy pan, turning until evenly browned.

2 Stir in the brandy, orange juice and scallions. Bring to a boil, then cover and simmer for 15 minutes, or until the chicken is tender and the juices run clear, not pink, when pierced.

3 Blend the cornstarch with a little water then mix into the ricotta. Stir this into the sauce and stir over moderate heat until boiling.

4 Adjust the seasoning and serve with boiled rice or pasta and green salad.

COOK'S TIP
Cornstarch stabilizes the ricotta and helps prevent it curdling.

Sage and Orange Sauce with Pork Fillet

Sage is often partnered with pork – there seems to be a natural affinity – and the addition of orange to the sauce balances the flavor.

Serves 4

INGREDIENTS
2 pork fillets, about 12 ounces each
2 teaspoons butter
½ cup dry sherry
¾ cup chicken broth
2 garlic cloves, very finely chopped
grated rind and juice of
  1 unwaxed orange
3 or 4 sage leaves, finely chopped
2 teaspoons cornstarch
salt and pepper
orange wedges and sage leaves,
  to garnish

pork

butter

dry sherry

chicken broth

garlic cloves

orange

sage leaves

cornstarch

NUTRITIONAL NOTES
PER PORTION:

CALORIES 330 **FAT** 14.6 g
SATURATED FAT 5.8 g **PROTEIN** 36.8 g
CARBOHYDRATE 4.4 g **FIBER** 0.1 g

1 Season the pork fillets lightly with salt and pepper. Melt the butter in a heavy flameproof casserole over medium-high heat, then add the meat and cook for 5–6 minutes, turning to brown all sides evenly.

2 Add the sherry, boil for about 1 minute, then add the broth, garlic, orange rind and sage. Bring to a boil and reduce the heat to low, then cover and simmer for 20 minutes, turning once. The meat is cooked if the juices run clear when the meat is pierced with a knife or a meat thermometer inserted into the thickest part of the meat registers 150°F.

3 Transfer the pork to a warmed plate and cover to keep warm.

4 Bring the sauce to a boil. Blend the cornstarch and orange juice and stir into the sauce, then boil gently over medium heat for a few minutes, stirring frequently, until the sauce is slightly thickened. Strain into a gravy cup or serving pitcher.

5 Slice the pork diagonally and pour the meat juices into the sauce. Spoon a little sauce over the pork and garnish with orange wedges and sage leaves. Serve the remaining sauce separately.

Cool Mint Raita

The ideal antidote to any spicy food, especially fiery Indian curries.

Serves 4

INGREDIENTS
6 large mint sprigs
1 small onion
$^1/_2$ cucumber
$1^1/_4$ cups plain yogurt
$^1/_2$ tsp salt
$^1/_2$ tsp sugar
pinch chili powder
mint sprig, to garnish

chili powder

mint

onion

cucumber

yogurt

1 Tear the mint leaves from their stems and chop finely.

2 Peel and very thinly slice the onion, separating it into rings. Cut the cucumber into $^1/_4$ in dice.

3 Mix together the mint, onion, cucumber, yogurt, salt and sugar. Spoon into a serving bowl and chill.

4 Just before serving sprinkle with chili powder and garnish with mint.

VARIATION
This also makes a deliciously fresh dip for crudites, for a creamier texture use strained yogurt, and add some crushed garlic for extra flavor. Serve with fresh vegetables or tortilla chips.

NUTRITIONAL NOTES
PER PORTION:

CALORIES 54 **FAT** 0.9 g
SATURATED FAT 0.5 g **PROTEIN** 4.4 g
CARBOHYDRATE 7.6 g **FIBER** 0.6 g

Chinese-style Sweet and Sour Sauce

A great family favorite that adds a taste of the Orient.

Serves 4

INGREDIENTS
1 carrot
1 green bell pepper
1 tbsp vegetable oil
1 small onion, chopped
1 garlic clove, crushed
$^1/_2$ in piece fresh ginger, peeled and grated
$^1/_2$ tbsp cornstarch
$1^1/_4$ cups white stock
2 tbsp tomato paste
1 tbsp dark brown sugar
2 tbsp white wine vinegar
2 tbsp rice wine or sherry
salt and pepper
stir-fried pork or chicken, to serve
rice or noodles, to serve
cucumber, to garnish

green bell pepper

white

white wine vinegar

onion

carrot

dark brown sugar

cornstarch

tomato paste

sherry

garlic

ginger

1 Peel the carrot and cut into matchstick-sized strips. Quarter the pepper, discard the stalks, seeds and membrane and cut into strips.

2 Heat the oil and fry the onion and garlic until soft but not brown. Add the carrot, pepper and ginger and cook for another minute. Remove from the heat.

NUTRITIONAL NOTES

PER PORTION:

CALORIES 85 **FAT** 3.0 g
SATURATED FAT 0.4 g **PROTEIN** 1.5 g
CARBOHYDRATE 12.6 g **FIBER** 1.5 g

3 Blend the cornfstarch with a little stock and add to the vegetables, together with the remaining ingredients.

4 Stir over a moderate heat until the mixture boils and thickens. Simmer uncovered for 2–3 minutes until the vegetables are just tender. Adjust the seasoning and serve with strips of stir-fried pork or chicken and with rice or noodles.

Tangy Orange Sauce (Sauce Bigarade)

A tangy orange sauce for roast duck and rich game. For a full mellow flavor it is best made with the rich roasting-pan juices – make sure that you pour off all the fat from the pan.

NUTRITIONAL NOTES

Per portion:

CALORIES 127 **FAT** 1.2 g
SATURATED FAT 0.4 g **PROTEIN** 2.2 g
CARBOHYDRATE 19.9 g **FIBER** 1.3 g

Serves 4 – 6

INGREDIENTS
roasting-pan juices
3 tbsp all-purpose flour
1¼ cups hot stock (preferably duck)
⅔ cup red wine
2 Temple oranges or 2 sweet oranges
   plus 2 tsp lemon juice
1 tbsp orange-flavored liqueur
2 tbsp red currant jelly
salt and pepper

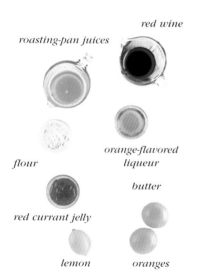

red wine

roasting-pan juices

flour

orange-flavored liqueur

butter

red currant jelly

lemon   *oranges*

1 Pour off any excess fat from the roasting pan, leaving the juices.

2 Sprinkle in the flour and cook, stirring constantly for 4 minutes or until lightly browned.

3 Remove from the heat, blend in the hot stock and wine. Reheat, bring to the boil, stirring constantly. Lower the heat and simmer for 5 minutes.

4 Meanwhile, using a citrus zester, peel the rind thinly from one orange. Squeeze the juice from both oranges.

5 Blanch the rind; place it in a small pan, cover with water and bring to a boil. Cook for 5 minutes, drain and add the rind to the sauce.

6 Add the orange juice, liqueur and jelly to the sauce, stirring until the jelly has dissolved. Season to taste and pour over the carved duckling or game.

SAUCES FOR PASTA

Tomato Sauce with Gnocchi and Tagliatelle

Serves 4–6

INGREDIENTS
1 pound mixed flavored tagliatelle
flour, for dusting
shavings of Parmesan cheese,
   to garnish

FOR THE SPINACH GNOCCHI
1 pound frozen chopped spinach
1 small onion, finely chopped
1 garlic clove, crushed
¼ teaspoon ground nutmeg
14 ounces low-fat cottage cheese
4 ounces dried white bread crumbs
3 ounces semolina or flour
2 ounces grated Parmesan cheese
3 egg whites
salt and pepper

FOR THE TOMATO SAUCE
1 onion, finely chopped
1 stick celery, finely chopped
1 red pepper, seeded and diced
1 garlic clove, crushed
⅔ cup vegetable stock
14 ounce can tomatoes
1 tablespoon tomato paste
2 teaspoons sugar
1 teaspoon dried oregano

1 To make the tomato sauce, put the chopped onion, celery, pepper and garlic into a non-stick pan. Add the stock, bring to a boil and cook for 5 minutes or until tender.

2 Add the tomatoes, tomato paste, sugar and oregano. Season to taste, bring to a boil and simmer for 30 minutes until thick, stirring occasionally.

3 Meanwhile, put the frozen spinach, onion and garlic into a saucepan, cover and cook until the spinach is defrosted. Remove the lid and increase the heat to remove excess water. Season with salt, pepper and nutmeg. Cool the spinach in a bowl, add the remaining ingredients and mix thoroughly.

celery

egg nutmeg garlic

onion

low-fat cottage cheese

flavored tagliatelle red pepper

grated Parmesan cheese spinach

dried white bread crumbs

vegetable stock

tomato paste tomatoes semolina

4 Shape the mixture into about 24 ovals with two dessertspoons and place them on a lightly floured tray. Place in the fridge for 30 minutes.

5 Have a large shallow pan of boiling, salted water ready. Cook the gnocchi in batches, for about 5 minutes. (The water should simmer gently and not boil.) As soon as the gnocchi rise to the surface, remove them with a slotted spoon and drain thoroughly.

6 Cook the tagliatelle in a large pan of boiling, salted water until *al dente*. Drain thoroughly. Transfer to warmed serving plates, top with gnocchi and spoon over the tomato sauce. Top with shavings of Parmesan cheese and serve at once.

NUTRITIONAL NOTES
PER PORTION:

ENERGY 789 calories **FAT** 10.9g
SATURATED FAT 3.7g **CHOLESTEROL** 20mg
CARBOHYDRATE 135g **FIBER** 8.1g

Milanese Sauce with Tagliatelle

Serves 4

INGREDIENTS
1 onion, finely chopped
1 stalk celery, finely chopped
1 red bell pepper, seeded and diced
1–2 garlic cloves, crushed
²/₃ cup vegetable stock
14 ounce can tomatoes
1 tbsp tomato paste
2 teaspoons sugar
1 teaspoon mixed dried herbs
12 ounces tagliatelle
4 ounces button mushrooms, sliced
4 tablespoons white wine
4 ounces lean cooked ham, diced
salt and ground black pepper
1 tablespoon chopped fresh parsley,
    to garnish

garlic

celery

tagliatelle

red pepper

onion

lean
cooked
ham

button
mushrooms

parsley

tomato
paste

vegetable stock

tomatoes

white wine

1 Put the chopped onion, celery, pepper and garlic into a non-stick pan. Add the stock, bring to a boil and cook for 5 minutes or until tender.

2 Add the tomatoes, tomato paste, sugar and herbs. Season with salt and pepper. Bring to a boil, simmer for 30 minutes until thick. Stir occasionally.

3 Cook the pasta in a large pan of boiling, salted water until al dente. Drain thoroughly.

4 Put the mushrooms into a pan with the white wine, cover and cook for 3–4 minutes until tender and all the wine has evaporated.

5 Add the mushrooms and diced ham to the tomato sauce. Reheat gently.

6 Transfer the pasta to a warmed serving dish and spoon on the sauce. Garnish with parsley.

NUTRITIONAL NOTES
Per portion:

ENERGY 405 calories **FAT** 3.5g
SATURATED FAT 0.8g **CHOLESTEROL** 17mg
CARBOHYDRATE 77g **FIBER** 4.5g

Mixed Bean Chili Sauce

Serves 6

INGREDIENTS
1 onion, finely chopped
1–2 garlic cloves, crushed
1 large green chili, seeded
   and chopped
²⁄₃ cup vegetable stock
14 ounce can chopped tomatoes
2 tablespoons tomato paste
¹⁄₂ cup red wine
1 teaspoon dried oregano
7 ounces green beans, sliced
14 ounce can red kidney
   beans, drained
14 ounce can cannellini
   beans, drained
14 ounce can chick-peas, drained
1 pound spaghetti
salt and ground black pepper

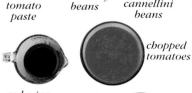

spaghetti   *onion*

green chili   *garlic*   *green beans*

tomato paste   *red kidney beans*   *cannellini beans*

red wine   *chopped tomatoes*

vegetable stock   *chick-peas*

1 To make the sauce, put the chopped onion, garlic and chili into a non-stick pan with the stock. Bring to a boil and cook for 5 minutes until tender.

2 Add the tomatoes, tomato paste, wine, seasoning and oregano. Bring to a boil, cover and simmer the sauce for 20 minutes.

NUTRITIONAL NOTES
PER PORTION:

ENERGY 431 calories **FAT** 3.6g
SATURATED FAT 0.2g **CHOLESTEROL** 0mg
CARBOHYDRATE 82g **FIBER** 9.9g

3 Cook the green beans in boiling, salted water for about 5–6 minutes until tender. Drain thoroughly.

4 Add all the beans to the sauce and simmer for 10 more minutes. Cook the spaghetti in a large pan of boiling, salted water until *al dente*. Drain thoroughly. Transfer to a serving dish and top with the chili beans.

Black Olive and Mushroom Sauce with Spaghetti

A rich pungent sauce topped with sweet cherry tomatoes.

Serves 4

INGREDIENTS
1 tsp olive oil
1 garlic clove, chopped
8 oz mushrooms, chopped
2 oz black olives, pitted
2 tbsp chopped fresh parsley
1 fresh red chili, seeded and chopped
1 lb spaghetti
8 oz cherry tomatoes
slivers of Parmesan cheese,
   to serve (optional)

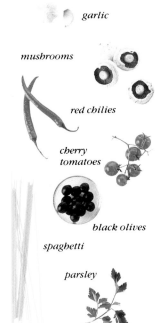

garlic

mushrooms

red chilies

cherry tomatoes

black olives

spaghetti

parsley

1 Heat the oil in a large pan. Add the garlic and cook for 1 minute. Add the mushrooms, cover, and cook over a medium heat for 5 minutes.

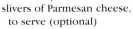

2 Place the mushrooms in a blender or food processor with the olives, parsley and red chili. Blend until smooth.

NUTRITIONAL NOTES
PER PORTION:

CALORIES 425 **FAT** 4.7 g
SATURATED FAT 0.7 g **PROTEIN** 15.3 g
CARBOHYDRATE 85.6 g **FIBER** 5.1 g

3 Cook the pasta following the instructions on the side of the package until *al dente*. Drain well and return to the pan. Add the olive mixture and toss together until the pasta is well coated. Cover and keep warm.

4 Heat an ungreased frying pan and shake the cherry tomatoes around until they start to split (about 2–3 minutes). Serve the pasta topped with the tomatoes and garnished with slivers of Parmesan, if desired.

Creamy Pea Sauce with Pasta, Asparagus and Broad Beans

A creamy pea sauce makes a wonderful combination with crunchy young vegetables.

Serves 4

INGREDIENTS
1 tbsp olive oil
1 garlic clove, crushed
6 scallions, sliced
1 cup fresh or frozen baby peas, defrosted
12 oz fresh young asparagus
2 tbsp chopped fresh sage, plus extra leaves, to garnish
finely grated rind of 2 lemons
1¾ cups fresh vegetable stock or water
8 oz fresh or frozen broad beans, defrosted
1 lb tagliatelle
4 tbsp low-fat yogurt

lemon

garlic

asparagus

broad beans

peas

yogurt

tagliatelle

sage

scallions

1 Heat the oil in a pan. Add the garlic and scallions and cook gently for 2–3 minutes until softened.

2 Add the peas and ⅓ of the asparagus, together with the sage, lemon rind and stock or water. Bring to a boil, reduce the heat and simmer for 10 minutes until tender. Purée in a blender until smooth.

3 Meanwhile remove the outer skins from the broad beans and discard.

4 Cut the remaining asparagus into 2 in lengths trimming off any tough fibrous stems, and blanch in boiling water for 2 minutes.

5 Cook the tagliatelle following the instructions on the side of the package until *al dente*. Drain well.

NUTRITIONAL NOTES
PER PORTION:

CALORIES 522 **FAT** 6.9 g
SATURATED FAT 0.9 g **PROTEIN** 23.8 g
CARBOHYDRATE 97.1 g **FIBER** 11.2 g

COOK'S TIP

Frozen peas and beans have been suggested here to cut down the preparation time, but the dish tastes even better if you use fresh young vegetables when in season.

6 Add the cooked asparagus and shelled beans to the sauce and reheat. Stir in the yogurt and toss into the tagliatelle. Garnish with a few extra sage leaves and serve.

Provençal Sauce with Pappardelle

Serves 4

INGREDIENTS
2 small purple onions, peeled
²/₃ cup vegetable stock
1–2 garlic cloves, crushed
4 tablespoons red wine
2 zucchini, sliced lengthwise
1 yellow bell pepper, seeded
    and sliced
14 ounce can tomatoes
2 teaspoons fresh thyme
1 teaspoon sugar
12 ounces pappardelle
salt and ground black pepper
fresh thyme and 6 black olives,
    stoned and coarsely chopped,
    to garnish

zucchini

*yellow
bell pepper*

purple onions

pappardelle

thyme

garlic

*black
olives*

tomatoes

vegetable stock

red wine

1 Cut each onion into eight wedges through the root end, so that they hold together during cooking. Put into a saucepan with the stock and garlic. Bring to the boil, cover and simmer for 5 minutes until tender.

2 Add the red wine, zucchini, yellow pepper, tomatoes, thyme, sugar and seasoning. Bring to a boil and cook gently for 5–7 minutes, shaking the pan occasionally to coat the vegetables with the sauce. (Do not overcook the vegetables, as they are much nicer if they are slightly crunchy.)

3 Cook the pasta in a large pan of boiling, salted water until *al dente*. Drain thoroughly.

NUTRITIONAL NOTES
PER PORTION:

ENERGY 369 calories **FAT** 2.5g
SATURATED FAT 0.4g **CHOLESTEROL** 0mg
CARBOHYDRATE 75g **FIBER** 4.3g

4 Transfer the pasta to a warmed serving dish and top with the vegetables. Garnish with fresh thyme and chopped black olives.

Tomato and Tuna Sauce with Pasta Shells

Serves 6

INGREDIENTS

1 medium onion, finely chopped
1 stick celery, finely chopped
1 red bell pepper, seeded and diced
1 garlic clove, crushed
²/₃ cup chicken stock
14 ounce can chopped tomatoes
1 tablespoon tomato paste
2 teaspoons caster sugar
1 tablespoon chopped fresh basil
1 tablespoon chopped fresh parsley
1 pound dried pasta shells
14 ounce canned tuna packed in
    water, drained
2 tablespoons capers in
    vinegar, drained
salt and ground black pepper

celery
canned tuna
tomato paste
capers
garlic
bell pepper
stock
onion
chopped tomatoes
basil
parsley

1 Put the chopped onion, celery, pepper and garlic into a non-stick pan. Add the stock, bring to a boil and cook for 5 minutes or until the stock is reduced almost completely.

2 Add the tomatoes, tomato paste, sugar and herbs. Season to taste and bring to a boil. Simmer for 30 minutes until thick, stirring occasionally.

NUTRITIONAL NOTES

PER PORTION:

ENERGY 369 calories **FAT** 2.1g
SATURATED FAT 0.4g **CHOLESTEROL** 34mg
CARBOHYDRATE 65g **FIBER** 4g

3 Meanwhile cook the pasta in a large pan of boiling, salted water according to package instructions. Drain thoroughly and transfer to a warm serving dish.

4 Flake the tuna into large chunks and add to the sauce with the capers. Heat gently for 1–2 minutes, pour over the pasta, toss gently and serve at once.

Bolognese Sauce with Ravioli

Serves 6

INGREDIENTS

8 ounces low-fat cottage cheese
2 tablespoons grated Parmesan cheese, plus extra for serving
1 egg white, beaten, including extra for brushing
¼ teaspoon ground nutmeg
1 recipe pasta dough
flour, for dusting
1 medium onion, finely chopped
1 garlic clove, crushed
⅔ cup beef stock
12 ounces extra lean ground beef
½ cup red wine
2 tablespoons tomato paste
14 ounce can chopped tomatoes
½ tsp chopped fresh rosemary
¼ tsp ground allspice
salt and ground black pepper

nutmeg

onion

ground beef

stock

tomato purée

low-fat cottage cheese

red wine

Parmesan cheese

chopped tomatoes

egg

rosemary

garlic

1 To make the filling mix the cottage cheese, grated Parmesan, egg white, seasoning and nutmeg together thoroughly.

2 Roll the pasta into thin sheets and place a small teaspoon of filling along the pasta in rows 2 inches apart.

3 Moisten between the filling with beaten egg white. Lay a second sheet of pasta lightly over the top and press between each pocket to remove any air and seal firmly.

4 Cut into rounds with a fluted ravioli or pastry cutter. Transfer to a floured cloth and let rest for at least 30 minutes before cooking.

5 To make the Bolognese sauce cook the onion and garlic in the stock for 5 minutes or until all the stock is reduced. Add the beef and cook quickly to brown, breaking up the meat with a fork. Add the wine, tomato paste, chopped tomatoes, rosemary and allspice, bring to a boil and simmer for 1 hour. Adjust the seasoning to taste.

6 Cook the ravioli in a large pan of boiling, salted water for 4–5 minutes. (Cook in batches to stop them from sticking together.) Drain thoroughly. Serve topped with Bolognese sauce. Serve grated Parmesan cheese separately.

NUTRITIONAL NOTES

PER PORTION:

ENERGY 321 calories **FAT** 8.8g
SATURATED FAT 3g **CHOLESTEROL** 158mg
CARBOHYDRATE 32g **FIBER** 2g

Cheese Sauce & Macaroni

Serves 4

INGREDIENTS

1 medium onion, chopped
²/₃ cup vegetable or chicken stock
1 ounce low-fat margarine
1½ ounces plain flour
¼ cup skim milk
2 ounces reduced-fat Cheddar
    cheese, grated
1 teaspoon mustard
8 ounces quick-cook macaroni
4 smoked turkey bacon slices,
    cut in half
2–3 firm tomatoes, sliced
a few fresh basil leaves
1 tablespoon grated Parmesan
    cheese
salt and ground black pepper

tomatoes

onion

smoked turkey
bacon

basil   Parmesan
cheese

low-fat
margarine

macaroni

flour

stock

skim milk

Cheddar
cheese

1 Put the onion and stock into a non-stick frying pan. Bring to a boil, stirring occasionally and cook for 5–6 minutes or until the stock has reduced entirely and the onions are transparent.

2 Put the margarine, flour, milk, and seasoning into a pan and whisk together over the heat until thickened and smooth. Remove from the heat and add the cheeses, mustard and onions.

NUTRITIONAL NOTES
PER PORTION:

ENERGY 152 calories FAT 2.8g
SATURATED FAT 0.7g CHOLESTEROL 12mg
CARBOHYDRATE 23g FIBER 1.1g

3 Cook the macaroni in a large pan of boiling, salted water for 6 minutes or according to the instructions on the package. Drain thoroughly and stir into the sauce. Transfer the macaroni to a shallow ovenproof dish.

4 Layer the turkey bacon and tomatoes on top of the macaroni and cheese, sprinkling the basil leaves over the tomatoes. Lightly sprinkle with Parmesan cheese and broil to lightly brown the top.

Watercress and Herb Sauce with Shrimp and Pasta

Serves 4–6

INGREDIENTS

4 anchovy fillets, drained
4 tablespoons skim milk
8 ounces squid
1 tablespoon chopped capers
1 tablespoon chopped cornichons
1–2 garlic cloves, crushed
$2/3$ cup low-fat plain yogurt
2–3 tablespoons reduced-fat
    mayonnaise
squeeze of lemon juice
2 ounces watercress, finely chopped
2 tablespoons chopped fresh parsley
2 tablespoons chopped fresh basil
12 ounces fusilli
12 ounces peeled shrimp
salt and ground black pepper

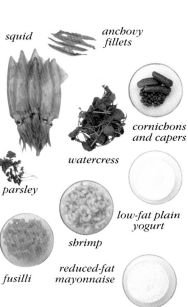

squid
anchovy fillets
cornichons and capers
watercress
parsley
low-fat plain yogurt
shrimp
fusilli
reduced-fat mayonnaise
garlic *lemon* *basil*

1 Put the anchovies into a small bowl and cover with the skim milk. Leave to soak for 10 minutes to remove the oil and strong salty flavor. Pull the head from the body of each squid and remove the quill. Peel outer speckled skin from the bodies. Cut the tentacles from the heads and rinse under cold water. Cut into 1/4-inch rings.

2 To make the dressing, mix the capers, cornichons, garlic, yogurt, mayonnaise, lemon juice and fresh herbs in a bowl. Drain and chop the anchovies. Add to the dressing with the seasoning.

3 Drop the squid rings into a large pan of boiling, salted water. Lower the heat and simmer for 1–2 minutes. (Do not overcook or the squid will become tough.) Remove with a slotted spoon. Cook the pasta in the same water according to the instructions on the package. Drain thoroughly.

4 Mix the shrimp and squid into the dressing in a large bowl. Add the pasta, toss and serve warm or cold as a salad.

NUTRITIONAL NOTES

PER PORTION:

ENERGY 502 calories **FAT** 6.9g
SATURATED FAT 1.1g **CHOLESTEROL** 72mg
CARBOHYDRATE 71g **FIBER** 3.2g

Spinach Sauce with Seafood Pasta Shells

You'll need very large pasta shells, measuring about 1½ in long for this dish; don't try stuffing smaller shells – it's much too fussy!

Serves 4

NUTRITIONAL NOTES

PER SERVING:

CALORIES 399 PROTEIN 32.69 g
FAT 12.79 g SATURATED FAT 5.81 g
CARBOHYDRATE 40.75 g FIBER 3.31 g
ADDED SUGAR 0 SODIUM 3.59 g

INGREDIENTS

1 tbsp low fat spread
8 scallions, finely sliced
6 tomatoes
32 large dried pasta shells
1 cup low fat cream cheese
6 tbsp skim milk
pinch of freshly grated nutmeg
8 oz shrimp
6 oz can white crabmeat, drained and flaked
4 oz frozen chopped spinach, thawed and drained
salt and freshly ground black pepper

scallions

shrimp

pasta shells

crabmeat

spinach

tomatoes

1 Preheat the oven to 300°F. Melt the low fat spread in a small saucepan and gently cook the scallions for 3-4 minutes, or until softened.

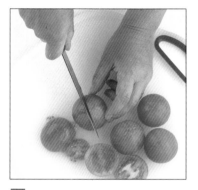

2 Plunge the tomatoes into a saucepan of boiling water for 1 minute, then into a saucepan of cold water. Slip off the skins. Halve the tomatoes, remove the seeds and cores and roughly chop the flesh.

3 Cook the pasta shells in lightly salted boiling water for about 10 minutes, or until *al dente*. Drain well.

4 Put the low fat cream cheese and skim milk into a saucepan and heat gently, stirring until blended. Season with salt, freshly ground black pepper and a pinch of nutmeg. Measure 2 tbsp of the sauce into a bowl.

5 Add the scallions, tomatoes, shrimp, and crabmeat to the bowl. Mix well. Spoon the filling into the shells and place in a single layer in a shallow ovenproof dish. Cover with foil and cook in the preheated oven for 10 minutes.

6 Stir the spinach into the remaining sauce. Bring to a boil and simmer gently for 1 minute, stirring all the time. Drizzle over the pasta shells and serve hot.

Tomato and Cilantro Salsa

Salsa is Spanish for sauce, but elsewhere it has come to mean a side dish of finely chopped vegetables or fruits, which really enhances the meals it accompanies.

Serves 6

INGREDIENTS
6 medium tomatoes
1 green chili
2 scallions, chopped
4 in length cucumber, peeled and diced
2 tbsp lemon juice
2 tbsp fresh cilantro, chopped
1 tbsp fresh parsley, chopped
salt and pepper

basil

tomatoes

orange pepper

parsley

lemon

scallions

cilantro

garlic

cucumber

capers

green chili

1 Cut a small cross in the stalk end of each tomato. Place in a bowl and cover with boiling water.

2 After 30 seconds or as soon as the skins split, drain and plunge into cold water. Gently slide off the skins. Quarter the tomatoes, remove the seeds and dice the flesh.

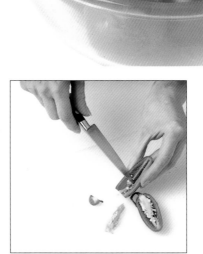

3 Halve the chili, remove the stalk, seeds and membrane, and chop finely.

4 Mix together all the ingredients and transfer to a serving bowl. Chill for 1–2 hours before serving.

NUTRITIONAL NOTES

PER PORTION:

CALORIES 14 **FAT** 0.3 g
SATURATED FAT 0 **PROTEIN** 0.8 g
CARBOHYDRATE 2.4 g **FIBER** 0.9 g

VARIATIONS

Tomato and Caper Salsa:
Prepare the tomatoes and stir in
the onion and lemon juice. Add
six torn sprigs of basil and 1 tbsp
coarsely chopped capers. Season
to taste.

Tomato and Roast Pepper Salsa:
Prepare 4 tomatoes and stir in the
chili, onion and herbs. Add a
roasted, peeled and diced orange
bell pepper and a crushed garlic
clove. Season to taste.

Roasted Pepper and Ginger Salsa

Char-broiling to remove the skins will take away any bitterness from the peppers.

Serves 6

NUTRITIONAL NOTES
PER PORTION:

CALORIES 33 **FAT** 0.6 g
SATURATED FAT 0 **PROTEIN** 1.4 g
CARBOHYDRATE 5.9 g **FIBER** 1.6 g

INGREDIENTS
1 large red bell pepper
1 large yellow bell pepper
1 large orange bell pepper
1 in piece fresh ginger
1/2 tsp coriander seeds
1 tsp cumin seeds
1 small garlic clove
2 tbsp lime or lemon juice
1 small red onion, finely chopped
2 tbsp chopped fresh cilantro
1 tsp chopped fresh thyme
salt and pepper

red pepper

thyme

yellow pepper

coriander and cumin seeds

garlic

orange pepper

lime

ginger

cilantro

1 Quarter the peppers and remove the stalk, seeds and membranes.

2 Grill the quarters, skin side up, until charred and blistered. Rub away the skins and slice very finely.

3 Peel or scrape the ginger and chop coarsely.

4 Over a moderate heat, gently dry-fry the spices for 30 seconds to 1 minute, making sure they don't burn.

5 Crush the spices in a mortar and pestle. Add the ginger and garlic and continue to work to a pulp. Work in the lime or lemon juice.

6 Mix together the peppers, spice mixture, onion and herbs. Season to taste and spoon into a serving bowl. Chill for 1–2 hours before serving as an accompaniment to barbecued meats or kebabs.

Melon and Chili Salsa with Grilled Chicken

This dish originates from Mexico. Its hot fruity flavors form the essence of Tex-Mex cooking.

Serves 4

NUTRITIONAL NOTES
PER PORTION:
CALORIES 184 **FAT** 5.5 g
SATURATED FAT 1.4 g **PROTEIN** 25.7 g
CARBOHYDRATE 8.6 g **FIBER** 0.8 g

INGREDIENTS
4 chicken breasts
pinch of celery salt and cayenne
    pepper combined
2 tsp vegetable oil
corn chips, to serve

FOR THE SALSA
10 oz watermelon
6 oz canteloupe melon
1 small red onion
1–2 green chilies
2 tbsp lime juice
4 tbsp chopped fresh cilantro
pinch of salt

green chilies

chicken breasts

red onion

lime

cilantro

canteloupe melon

watermelon

1 Preheat a moderate broiler. Slash the chicken breasts deeply to speed up the cooking time.

2 Season the chicken with celery salt and cayenne, brush with oil and broil for about 15 minutes.

3 To make the salsa, remove the rind and as many seeds as you can from the melons. Finely dice the flesh and put it into a bowl.

4 Finely chop the onion, split the chilies (discarding the seeds which contain most of the heat) and chop. Take care not to touch sensitive skin areas when handling cut chilies. Mix with the melon.

5 Add the lime juice and chopped cilantro, and season with a pinch of salt. Turn the salsa into a small bowl.

6 Arrange the grilled chicken on a plate and serve with the salsa and a handful of corn chips.

Fiery Citrus Salsa

This very unusual salsa makes a great marinade for shellfish and it is also delicious drizzled over barbecued meat.

NUTRITIONAL NOTES

PER PORTION:

CALORIES 30 **FAT** 0.1 g
SATURATED FAT 0 **PROTEIN** 0.7 g
CARBOHYDRATE 7.1 g **FIBER** 1.3 g

Serves 4

INGREDIENTS
1 orange
1 green apple
2 fresh red chilies
1 garlic clove
8 fresh mint leaves
juice of 1 lemon
salt and pepper

orange   *apple*

red chilies   *garlic*

mint   *lemon juice*

1 Slice the bottom off the orange so that it will stand upright on a cutting board. Using a sharp knife, remove the peel by slicing from the top to the bottom of the orange.

2 Hold the orange in one hand over a bowl. Slice toward the middle of the fruit, to one side of a segment, and then gently twist the knife to ease the segment away from the membrane and out of the orange. Repeat to remove all the segments. Squeeze any juice from the remaining membrane into the bowl.

3 Peel the apple, slice it into wedges and remove the core.

4 Halve the chilies and remove their seeds, then place them in a blender or food processor with the orange segments and juice, apple wedges, garlic and fresh mint.

5 Process until smooth. Then, with the motor running, pour in the lemon juice.

6 Season to taste with a little salt and pepper. Pour into a bowl or small pitcher and serve immediately.

VARIATION

If you're feeling really fiery, don't seed the chilies! They will make the salsa particularly hot and zesty.

Aromatic Peach and Cucumber Salsa

Angostura bitters add an unusual and very pleasing flavor to this salsa. Distinctive, sweet-tasting mint complements chicken and other main meat dishes.

Serves 4

INGREDIENTS
2 peaches
1 small cucumber
½ tsp Angostura bitters
1 tbsp olive oil
2 tsp fresh lemon juice
2 tbsp chopped fresh mint
salt and pepper

peaches   *small cucumber*

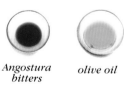

Angostura bitters   *olive oil*

lemon juice   *mint*

COOK'S TIP
The texture of the peach and the crispness of the cucumber will fade fairly rapidly, so try to prepare this salsa as close to serving time as possible.

1 Using a small sharp knife, carefully score a line right around the circumference of each peach, cutting just through the skin.

2 Bring a large pan of water to a boil. Add the peaches and blanch them for 60 seconds. Drain and briefly refresh in cold water.

3 Peel off and discard the skin. Halve the peaches and remove their pits. Finely dice the flesh and place in a bowl.

4 Cut the ends off the cucumber, then finely dice the flesh and stir it into the peaches.

5 Stir the Angostura bitters, olive oil and lemon juice together and then stir this dressing into the peach mixture.

NUTRITIONAL NOTES
PER PORTION:

CALORIES 47 **FAT** 2.9 g
SATURATED FAT 0.4 g **PROTEIN** 0.9 g
CARBOHYDRATE 4.8 g **FIBER** 0.9 g

6 Stir in the mint with salt and pepper to taste. Chill and serve within 1 hour.

Mango and Red Onion Salsa

A very simple salsa, enlivened by the addition of passion fruit pulp.

NUTRITIONAL NOTES
PER PORTION:

CALORIES 61 **FAT** 0.3 g
SATURATED FAT 0 **PROTEIN** 1.1 g
CARBOHYDRATE 14.5 g **FIBER** 2.9 g

Serves 4

INGREDIENTS
1 large ripe mango
1 red onion
2 passion fruit
6 large fresh basil leaves
juice of 1 lime, to taste
sea salt

mango   *red onion*

passion   *basil*
fruit

lime juice

1 Holding the mango upright on a cutting board, use a large knife to slice the flesh away from either side of the large flat pit in two portions.

2 Using a smaller knife, trim away any flesh still clinging to the top and bottom of the pit.

3 Score the flesh of the mango halves deeply, taking care to avoid cutting through the skin. Make parallel incisions about ½ in apart; turn and cut lines in the opposite direction. Carefully turn the skin inside out so the flesh stands out like porcupine spikes. Slice the dice away from the skin.

4 Finely chop the red onion and place it in a bowl with the mango.

5 Halve the passion fruit, scoop out the seeds and pulp, and add to the mango mixture.

6 Tear the basil leaves coarsely and stir them into the salsa with lime juice and a little sea salt to taste. Serve immediately.

VARIATION
Corn kernels are a delicious addition to this salsa.

Hot Plum Sauce with Floating Islands

An unusual, low fat dessert that is simpler to make than it looks. The plum sauce can be made in advance, then reheated just before you cook the meringues.

NUTRITIONAL NOTES
PER PORTION:

CALORIES 91 **FAT** 0.3 g
SATURATED FAT 0 **PROTEIN** 2.1 g
CARBOHYDRATE 21.2 g **FIBER** 1.7 g

Serves 4

INGREDIENTS
1 lb red plums
1¼ cups apple juice
2 egg whites
2 tbsp apple juice concentrate
freshly grated nutmeg

apple juice

red plums

eggs

apple juice concentrate

nutmeg

1 Halve the plums and remove the pits. Place them in a wide pan, with the apple juice.

2 Bring to a boil and then cover and let simmer gently until the plums are tender.

3 Meanwhile, place the egg whites in a clean, dry bowl and whisk them until they hold soft peaks.

4 Gradually whisk in the apple juice syrup, whisking until the meringue holds fairly firm peaks.

5 Using a tablespoon, scoop the meringue mixture into the gently simmering plum sauce. You may need to cook the "islands" in two batches.

6 Cover and let simmer gently for 2–3 minutes, until the meringues are just set. Serve immediately, sprinkled with a little freshly ground nutmeg.

Apricot Sauce with Coconut Dumplings

These delicate little dumplings are very simple to make and cook in minutes. The sharp flavor of the sauce offsets the creamy dumplings beautifully.

Serves 4

INGREDIENTS
FOR THE DUMPLINGS
⅓ cup farmer's cheese
1 egg white
2 tbsp low fat spread
1 tbsp light brown sugar
2 tbsp self-raising whole
  wheat flour
finely grated rind of ½ lemon
2 tbsp shredded coconut,
  toasted

FOR THE SAUCE
8 oz can apricot halves in
  natural juice
1 tbsp lemon juice

Half-fill a steamer with boiling water and put it on to boil. Alternatively, place a heatproof plate over a pan of boiling water.

2 Beat together the cottage cheese, egg white and low-fat spread until they are evenly mixed.

apricot halves

shredded coconut

whole wheat flour

lemon

cottage cheese

low-fat spread

egg

light brown sugar

3 Stir in the sugar, flour, lemon rind and coconut, mixing everything evenly to a fairly firm dough.

4 Place 8–12 spoonfuls of the mixture in the steamer or on the plate, leaving a space between them.

5 Cover the steamer or pan tightly with a lid or a plate and steam for about 10 minutes, until the dumplings have risen and are firm to the touch.

6 Meanwhile, purée the can of apricots and stir in the lemon juice. Pour into a small pan and heat until boiling, then serve with the dumplings. Serve with extra coconut sprinkled on top.

Nectarine Sauce with Latticed Peaches

An elegant dessert; it certainly doesn't look low in fat, but it really is.

NUTRITIONAL NOTES
Per portion:
CALORIES 202 **FAT** 10.8 g
SATURATED FAT 4.3 g **PROTEIN** 4.9 g
CARBOHYDRATE 23.1 g **FIBER** 2.3 g

Serves 6

INGREDIENTS
FOR THE PASTRY
1 cup all-purpose flour
3 tbsp butter or sunflower margarine
3 tbsp low fat plain yogurt
2 tbsp orange juice
skim milk

FOR THE FILLING
3 ripe peaches or nectarines
3 tbsp ground almonds
2 tbsp low fat plain yogurt
finely grated rind of 1 small orange
¼ tsp almond extract

FOR THE SAUCE
1 ripe peach or nectarine
3 tbsp orange juice

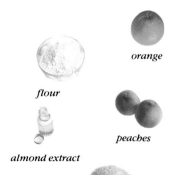

orange

flour

almond extract

peaches

ground almonds

1 For the pastry, sift the flour into a bowl and, using your fingertips, rub in the butter or margarine evenly. Stir in the yogurt and orange juice to bind the mixture to a firm dough.

2 Roll out about half the pastry thinly and use a cookie cutter to stamp out rounds about 3 in in diameter, slightly larger than the circumference of the peaches. Place on a lightly greased baking sheet.

3 Skin the peaches, halve and remove the pits. Mix together the almonds, yogurt, orange rind and almond extract. Spoon into the hollows of each peach half and place, cut side down, on to the pastry rounds.

4 Roll out the remaining pastry thinly and cut into thin strips. Arrange the strips over the peaches to form a lattice, brushing with milk to secure firmly. Trim off the ends neatly.

5 Chill in the refrigerator for 30 minutes. Preheat the oven to 400°F Brush with milk and bake for 15–18 minutes, until golden brown.

6 For the sauce, skin the peach or nectarine and halve it to remove the pit. Place the flesh in a food processor, with the orange juice, and purée it until smooth. Serve the peaches hot, with the peach sauce spooned around.

Lemon and Lime Sauce

A tangy, refreshing sauce to end a heavy meal, it goes well with crepes or fruit tarts.

Serves 4

INGREDIENTS
1 lemon
2 limes
$^1/_4$ cup superfine sugar
$1^1/_2$ tbsp arrowroot
$1^1/_4$ cups water
lemon balm or mint, to garnish

limes

arrowroot

*superfine
sugar*

lemon

1 Using a citrus zester, peel the rinds thinly from the lemon and limes. Squeeze the juice from the fruit.

2 Place the rind in a pan, cover with water and bring to the boil. Drain through a strainer and reserve the rind.

3 In a small bowl, mix a little sugar with the arrowroot. Blend in enough water to make a smooth paste. Heat the remaining water, pour in the arrowroot, and stir constantly until the sauce boils and thickens.

4 Stir in the remaining sugar, citrus juice and reserved rind, and serve hot with freshly made crepes. Decorate with lemon balm or mint.

VARIATION

This sauce can also be made with orange and lemon rind if you prefer, and makes an ideal accompaniment for a rich orange or mandarin cheesecake.

NUTRITIONAL NOTES
PER PORTION:

CALORIES 75 **FAT** 0.1 g
SATURATED FAT 0 **PROTEIN** 0.3 g
CARBOHYDRATE 19.6 g **FIBER** 0

Raspberry Sauce with Baked Peaches

This tart fat-free fruit coulis is exceedingly quick to make – add a little liqueur for a special occasion.

Serves 4

INGREDIENTS
1 ounce low fat spread, at
 room temperature
2 ounces sugar
1 small egg, beaten
2 ounces crushed amaretti biscuits
6 ripe peaches

FOR THE SAUCE
1 cup raspberries
1 tablespoon confectioners' sugar
1 tablespoon fruit-flavored
 brandy (optional)

low fat
spread

sugar

small egg

amaretti
biscuits

ripe
peaches

raspberries

confectioners'
sugar

brandy

NUTRITIONAL NOTES
PER PORTION:

CALORIES 170 FAT 7.4 g
SATURATED FAT 1.1 g PROTEIN 4.4 g
CARBOHYDRATE 22 g FIBER 2.7 g

1 Preheat the oven to 350°F. Beat the low fat spread with the sugar until soft and fluffy. Beat in the egg. Add the crushed amaretti biscuits and beat just to blend well together.

2 Halve the peaches and remove the stones. With a spoon, scrape out some of the flesh from each peach half, slightly enlarging the hollow left by the pit. Reserve the excess peach flesh to use in the sauce.

3 Place the peach halves on a baking sheet (if necessary, secure with crumpled foil to keep them steady). Fill the hollow in each peach half with a little of the amaretti mixture.

4 Bake for about 30 minutes until the filling is puffed and golden and the peaches are very tender.

5 Meanwhile, to make the sauce, combine all the ingredients in a food processor or blender. Add the reserved peach flesh. Process until smooth. Press through a strainer set over a bowl to remove fibers and seeds. Let the peaches cool slightly. Place 2 peach halves on each plate and spoon round some of the sauce. Serve immediately.

Maple-yogurt Sauce with Poached Pears

An elegant dessert that is easier to make than it looks – poach the pears in advance, and have the yogurt sauce ready to spoon on to the plates just before you serve.

NUTRITIONAL NOTES

PER PORTION:

CALORIES 128 **FAT** 2.4 g
SATURATED FAT 1.4 g **PROTEIN** 2.0 g
CARBOHYDRATE 18.3 g **FIBER** 1.6 g

Serves 4

INGREDIENTS
FOR THE PASTRY
6 firm pears
1 tbsp lemon juice
1 cup sweet white wine
 or apple cider
thinly pared rind of 1 lemon
1 cinnamon stick
2 tbsp maple syrup
½ tsp arrowroot
⅔ cup strained plain yogurt

sweet white wine

yogurt

pears

maple syrup

lemon

arrowroot

cinnamon stick

1 Thinly peel the pears, leaving them whole and with stalks. Brush them with lemon juice, to prevent them from browning. Use a potato peeler or small knife to scoop out the core from the base of each pear.

2 Place the pears in a wide, heavy pan and pour over the wine, with enough cold water almost to cover the pears.

3 Add the lemon rind and cinnamon stick, and then bring to a boil. Reduce the heat, cover the pan and simmer the pears gently for 30–40 minutes, or until tender. Turn the pears occasionally so that they cook evenly. Lift out the pears carefully, draining them well.

4 Bring the liquid to a boil and boil uncovered until reduced to about ½ cup. Strain and add the maple syrup. Blend a little of the liquid with the arrowroot. Return to the pan and cook, stirring, until thick and clear. Cool.

5 Slice each pear about three-quarters of the way through, leaving the slices attached at the stem end. Fan each pear out on a serving plate.

6 Stir the 2 tbsp of the cooled syrup into the yogurt and spoon it around the pears. Drizzle with the remaining syrup and serve immediately.

Strawberry Sauce with Lemon Hearts

This speedy sweet sauce is totally fat free and makes a delicious accompaniment for these delicate lemon-flavored cheese hearts.

Serves 4

INGREDIENTS
¾ cup ricotta cheese
⅔ cup low fat yogurt
1 tbsp granulated artificial sweetener
finely grated rind of ½ lemon
2 tbsp lemon juice
2 tsp powdered gelatin
2 egg whites

FOR THE SAUCE
2 cups fresh or frozen and
    thawed strawberries
1 tbsp lemon juice

ricotta cheese

crème fraîche

lemon

powdered gelatin

eggs

strawberries

granulated artificial sweetener

I Beat the ricotta cheese until smooth. Stir in the low fat yogurt, sweetener and lemon rind.

2 Place the lemon juice in a small bowl and sprinkle the gelatin over it. Place the bowl over a pan of hot water and stir to dissolve the gelatin completely.

3 Quickly stir the gelatin into the cheese mixture, mixing it in evenly.

4 Beat the egg whites until they form soft peaks. Quickly fold them into the cheese mixture.

5 Spoon the mixture into six lightly oiled, individual heart-shaped molds and chill the moulds until set.

NUTRITIONAL NOTES
PER PORTION:

CALORIES 86 **FAT** 3.5 g
SATURATED FAT 0.1 g **PROTEIN** 6.7 g
CARBOHYDRATE 7.5 g **FIBER** 0.4 g

6 Place the strawberries and lemon juice in a blender and process until smooth. Pour the sauce on to serving plates and place the turned-out hearts on top. Decorate with slices of strawberry.

Red Currant and Raspberry Coulis

A dessert sauce for the height of summer to serve with light meringues and fruit sorbets. Make it especially pretty with a decoration of fresh flowers and leaves.

NUTRITIONAL NOTES
Per portion:

CALORIES 81 **FAT** 1.2 g
SATURATED FAT 0.6 g **PROTEIN** 1.7 g
CARBOHYDRATE 17.1 g **FIBER** 3.2 g

Serves 6

INGREDIENTS
8 oz red currants
1 lb raspberries
1/4 cup confectioner's sugar
1 tbsp cornstarch
juice of 1 orange
2 tbsp heavy cream

orange

confectioner's sugar

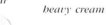

heavy cream

cornstarch

red currants and raspberries

1 Strip the red currants from their stalks using a fork. Place in a food processor or blender with the raspberries and sugar, and purée until it is smooth.

2 Press the mixture through a fine strainer into a saucepan and discard the seeds and pulp.

3 Blend the cornstarch with the orange juice, then stir into the fruit purée. Bring to the boil, stirring constantly, and cook for 1–2 minutes until smooth and thick. Leave until cold.

4 Spoon the sauce over each plate. Drip the cream from a teaspoon to make small dots evenly around the edge. Draw a toothpick through the dots to form heart shapes. Scoop or spoon sorbet into the middle and decorate with flowers.

INDEX